small business entrepreneur

...usiness

email: rory@burkepublishing.com

web site: www.burkepublishing.com

Rory Burke

 cosmic mba series

Small Business Entrepreneur
Rory Burke
ISBN 0-9582391-6-9

Published: 2006

Distributors: UK: Gazelle Books, email: sales@gazellebooks.co.uk
                USA: Partners Book Distributing, email: partnersbk@aol.com
                South Africa: Blue Weaver Marketing, email: orders@blueweaver.co.za
                Australia: Thames and Hudson, email: orders@thaust.com.au

DTP: Sandra Burke
Cover Design: Simon Larkin (Jag Graphics)
Sketches: Tang, Woric, Ingrid, Buddy Mendis, Rory Birk, Eddie Hoyle,
                Michael Glasswell
Printer: Everbest, China

Production notes: Page size (168 x 244 mm), Body Text (Adobe Garamond Pro 12 point), Chapter Headings (Helvetica, bold, 30 point), Subheadings (Helvetica, bold, 12 point), Software InDesign CS, Photoshop CS, Illustrator CS, CorelDRAW12, Dell and Mac notebook computers.

ISBN 0-9582391-6-9

Dedicated *to Deirdre, Chloe, Dexter, Poppy and Pippa, thank you for helping us with our logistics!*

Content

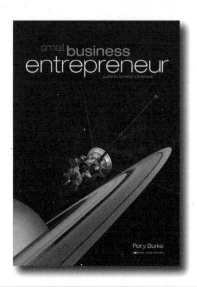

Entrepreneurs Toolkit	Small Business Entrepreneur
ISBN 0-9582391-4-2	ISBN 0-9582391-6-9
Entrepreneur BOK	Small Business Entrepreneur BOK
Entrepreneur Spiral	Staircase to Wealth
Do We Really Need Entrepreneurs?	What Type of Work?
Who Wants To Be An Entrepreneur?	Registering a Small Business
Entrepreneur Traits	Buying a Business
Creative Ideas	Buying a Franchise
Innovation Process	Family Business
Catching the Wave	Working From Home
Marketing	Selling Techniques
Networking	Customer Service
Negotiation	Outsourcing
Sources of Finance	Distribution
Managing Growth	Financial Statements
Risk Management	Business Plans

Cosmic MBA Series - content

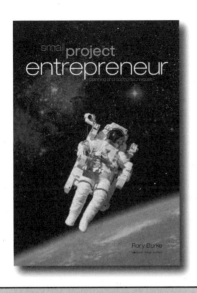

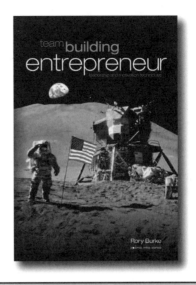

Small Project Entrepreneur	Team Building Entrepreneur
ISBN 0-9582391-1-8	ISBN 0-9582391-8-5
Small Project BOK	Team Building BOK
Product Life-Cycle	Teamwork
Plan and Control Cycle	Team Member Selection
WBS	Team Development Phases
CPM	Leadership Styles
Gantt Chart	Power to the People
Procurement	Motivating the Team
Resources	Delegation
Cash-Flow	Problem-Solving
Communication	Decision-Making
Quality Control Plan	Creativity and Innovation
Risk Management	Resistance to Change
Control (problem-solving)	Conflict Resolution
Crashing	Communication
Earned Value	Indoor Team Building
Computers	Outdoor Team Building
OBS / Matrix	Appendix - NASA Moon Landing

Foreword

It was 20 years ago today I started my own freight company. There were many reasons motivating me at the time, the main one was the frustration of working with people who would not change. And I didn't want to stay working for a company that was becoming increasingly obsolete.

I have always been intrigued and fascinated by people who do things differently. In hindsight, I can now see these people were entrepreneurs and they were the catalyst encouraging me to go out there and start my own business.

I believe **customer service** and **networking** are the key business skills needed to gain competitive advantage, because it is difficult to compete solely on product features (especially when your competitors are all offering very similar products), and you do not really want to compete on price as this reduces your profit margins.

Let me give you an example in my line of work. There are many other freight companies out there that can offer a similar freight service as ours, and there are many freight companies that are much cheaper (I am sure it is the same in your field). But none of them spend as much time and effort as I do engaging the customers – that is how I gain a distinct competitive advantage.

I visit my top five customers everyday – yes everyday!!! It may only be for a few minutes, but it confirms to them that I care about their business. And I make sure I visit all my other customers at least once every three months.

When I visit a company I don't just visit the CEO, I try and casually meet the key people at every level of the business. I usually park my car around the back of a company and walk in through the shop floor, this way I can network with the people at the workface – particularly those who are making and packing the goods. I am able to sort out any minor issues with them before they become a problem.

I have developed a symbiotic working relationship with many of my clients, and I am often asked by them to help with warehouse layouts, packaging systems, and time saving measures. As I visit so many companies I have seen what systems work and what arrangements don't work. I have even networked with my clients' clients to help them secure business.

To further cement my customer relationships I frequently give small gifts of rulers, golf balls and chocolates - I try and cater for both genders. These gifts cost little compared to the feeling of goodwill they can help to generate. I was even thinking of giving my valued customers a copy of Rory's entrepreneur book – but that might be going too far!

Rory's book on the *Small Business Entrepreneur* is an ideal book for people who want to start their own business, as it clearly sets out how to start a business together with the advantages and disadvantages of starting your own business. It is vitally important for the would be small business entrepreneurs to be aware of the pros and cons as there are many pitfalls out there which could end in tears.

However, the biggest pitfall of all is to go into business without basic small business management skills. This is why it is so important to read this book and start learning entrepreneurial skills so that you can make the most of the opportunities you have spotted and hit the ground running.

Russell Bodger
Freight Entrepreneur

Author's Note

With your head buzzing with innovative and creative ideas, welcome to the entrepreneur's world of spotting opportunities, networking and setting up new ventures. These desirable traits are increasingly seen as the difference between proactive businesses growing and creating wealth, and reactive businesses resisting change and 'hanging-in there' hoping to avoid the scrap heap.

Entrepreneurs are increasingly being acknowledged by governments as the driving force behind innovative change and job creation. In our deregulated and competitive world the small business entrepreneur can now compete on a level playing field with large corporations; it used to be *the big eat the small'* but now it is *'the fast assassinate the slow'*.

Business schools have responded to the demand for entrepreneurs by including entrepreneurship and business enterprise modules in many of their courses. The rationale being that when students graduate they can use these entrepreneurial skills to help establish their careers.

The growing wave of entrepreneurship made me realise there was an opportunity to write a series of books which focused on the entrepreneur's tools and techniques, their application, and the entrepreneur's behaviour and traits.

This is the second book on the launch pad - *Small Business Entrepreneur* - which focuses on the tools and techniques the entrepreneur can use to manage a small business on a day-to-day basis.

One of the unique features of *Small Business Entrepreneur* is a chapter on the *Staircase to Wealth* which outlines how an entrepreneur can gain leverage to create wealth.

Writing the cosmic MBA series has enabled me to subdivide the key management topics into a number of stand alone books linked by the common thread of entrepreneurship. In practise, no one management topic can really stand on its own for long - at some point the entrepreneur will need to use the other management skills.

Why call it the cosmic MBA series? Exploring the cosmos has always been the final frontier, and an excellent example of how man can use entrepreneurial skills to meet the ultimate challenge. This series is one small step to extend the library of small business entrepreneurial tools and techniques. And also a great opportunity to design some dynamic looking book covers (thanks NASA and Simon).

An **Instructor's Manual** is available for lecturers, with additional exercises and case studies, see <www.knowledgezone.net>. The Knowledge Zone web site has been set up to hold the educational resources for all our publications.

Acknowledgements: I have been researching these books for the past few years and wish to thank all the entrepreneurs and lecturers I have networked with around the world. I particularly wish to thank David Langford (University of Strathclyde), Marcus Jefferies (University of Newcastle), and Bruce Rodrigues (South Africa).

For proof reading I wish to thank Kirk Phillips, Kathleen Archibald and Jan Hamon, and for the inspirational foreword Russell and Laonie Bodger.

Rory Burke

Lifestyle Entrepreneur, currently
in the South Pacific 37 °S 175 °E

1
Small Business Entrepreneur Body of Knowledge

Starting your own business is an exciting prospect with the opportunity to be your own boss and shape your own destiny - and perhaps make a fortune in the process! The good news is, there are plenty of other people out there also setting up their own businesses and, therefore, information is widely available to guide you through the start up process and help you become established.

The experts advise that entrepreneurs setting up a small business for the first time should stick to the type of work they know best. This avoids having to learn a new trade plus small business management skills at the same time.

Entrepreneurs should also consider working in a field that interests them. This could include a hobby or interest that can be converted into a small business. This decision will pay dividends when having to work long hours to become established. It is reasonable to assume that the greater the enjoyment and passion in one's work, the greater the likelihood of success.

Budding entrepreneurs should discuss their intention to set up a small business with their immediate family as it is these close family members that are often negatively impacted by long working hours 24/7, tight cashflow (particularly during start up), and the emotional ups and downs as business is won and lost.

Entrepreneurs will benefit from discussing their small business proposals with other entrepreneurs and mentors who have already been through the start up process. The experienced entrepreneur (mentor) should be able to quickly highlight any obvious pitfalls and suggest how to navigate through the minefield of bureaucratic rules and regulations small businesses have to comply with.

If you have a secure well paid job, it is a brave decision to hand in your notice to start up your own small business with an unknown future. It is a bit like leaving home for the first time – you suddenly have to stand on your own two feet and fend for yourself. However, this challenge will enable you to grow much quicker as you gain real life experience at the coalface. Making mistakes is all part of the learning curve of life, particularly when your own money is on the line!

Setting up a business for the first time is one of the entrepreneur's most important decisions. There are many risks and uncertainties, but also big rewards - not just in terms of financial success, but also in sense of achievement and peer recognition.

1. Definition of SME

There is no single definition of a SME (Small and Medium sized Enterprise), mainly because of the wide diversity of small businesses. However, a small business is usually considered to be an independent business, managed by its owner or part-owners, with a small market share.

There are a number of definitions of SMEs produced by government departments around the world. The one thing they all seem to agree on is that size is best determined by the number of employees and turnover - see figure 1.1.

	Number of Employees	Turnover
Micro company	0-9 employees	Euro 2m
Small company	10-49 employees	Euro 10m
Medium company	50-249 employees	Euro 50m
Large company	over 250 employees	Euro <50m

Figure 1.1: SMEs

It should be noted that size is relevant to the sector of work. For instance, a firm of a given size could be small in relation to one sector (say in the oil industry where there are a number of extremely large corporations), whereas, a firm of similar proportions would be considered large in another sector (say in the fashion design industry where there are many small businesses).

SMEs are socially and economically important to society since they typically represent 99% of all enterprises in Europe and America, provide more than 50% of the employment and create most of the new jobs. Other interesting statistics include:

- small businesses create 3 out of every 4 new jobs in America
- small businesses typically produce more than 50% of the GDP
- small businesses typically invent 55% of all technical innovations.

Clearly, although SMEs do not feature in the Fortune 500 or FTSE 100 because individually they are too small, as a group, they are central to most economies, contributing to innovation, entrepreneurship, investment, employment and growth.

With deregulation and privatisation, the dominance of large nationalised industries is reducing. If free enterprise is allowed to develop, the future is with the smaller SMEs which are able to respond more quickly to technology changes and customer requirements (in their niche markets). In America 1 in 12 people have started a business, whereas in Britain, the figure is only 1 in 30 - Britain has some catching-up to do.

2. Small Business Entrepreneur BOK

Budding entrepreneurs thinking of starting their own business typically ask the following questions:

- What type of business should I set up?
- What does managing a small business involve?
- What business management skills do I need to learn?

These questions are best answered by first defining the Small Business Entrepreneur Body of Knowledge (BOK).

The body of knowledge of a profession is an inclusive term to describe the sum of knowledge within the profession. As with other professions, such as project management and accounting, the body of knowledge rests with the practitioners who use it. The small business entrepreneur body of knowledge identifies and describes the generally accepted practices for which there is widespread consensus of their value and usefulness, and also establishes a common lexicon of terms and expressions used within the profession.

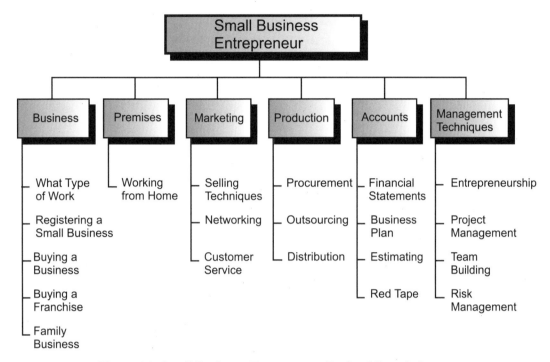

Figure 1.2: Small Business Entrepreneur Body of Knowledge

Although the small business entrepreneurial spirit has been a key feature in our evolution and industrial development, as a management profession it is still relatively new and has yet to formally define a small business entrepreneur body of knowledge. However, the many definitions of small business entrepreneur point to a number of knowledge areas or management topics which can be presented as a breakdown structure, see figure 1.2.

3. Business Knowledge Area

The business knowledge area covers the type of work the entrepreneur can pursue; whether they should buy an independent business, buy a franchise, stay in the family business or start from scratch.

What Type of Work? (**Chapter 3**): Statistically 80% of entrepreneurs start their first business in the field of their expertise, but there are also an increasing number of lifestyle entrepreneurs who try to develop their hobbies and interests into a business to provide an income.

Registering a Small Business (Chapter 4): There are a number of business structures suitable for SMEs, the chapter on *Registering a Business* discusses the three main options to consider:

- sole trader
- partnership
- limited company.

Each option has different implications with respect to liability, taxation, financial disclosure and administration. It is important to understand these different business structures so that you can make an informed decision.

Buying a Business (Chapter 5): Why go to all the trouble of setting up a business when you can buy an established business off the shelf? Buying a ready made business means you hit the ground running.

Buying a Franchise (Chapter 6): Buying a franchise business means you are buying the right to set up a business with a brand name and product which are already established in the market place. The big advantage of setting up a franchise is that it is usually a much faster way of expanding your business compared with starting from scratch and growing it on your own.

Family Business (Chapter 7): Many small businesses want to '*keep it in the family*', but keeping it in the family can be a double edged sword. On the one hand it appears to be a secure job on a plate, but on the other hand, the family business may limit the budding entrepreneur's scope for exploring new opportunities, investment and growth.

4. Premises Knowledge Area

The premises knowledge area discusses where you conduct your business - this could be an office, factory, warehouse, garage, shed, or spare room. This is a major consideration when setting up a new business. While you want to keep the costs down until the sales take-off, you do not want to dilute the opportunity you are pursuing by starting in an inappropriate type of premises.

Working from Home (Chapter 8): Working from home is becoming more popular, and increasingly becoming more feasible with new technology, new types of products and new ways to do business.

5. Sales and Marketing Knowledge Area

Selling Techniques (Chapter 9): The sales and marketing knowledge area covers the sales and marketing of a small business. The sales and marketing functions are two sides of the same coin, as one leads to the other. Marketing is the management function to make people aware of the company and its products and create an interest, while the sales function closes the deal and makes the sale.

Networking *(Entrepreneurs Toolkit)*: Networking and negotiation fall under the marketing umbrella. Networking skills enable the entrepreneur to use the back door to gain access to ideas, information and resources, while negotiation skills enable the entrepreneur to get a better deal.

Customer Service (Chapter 10): As products become increasingly complicated and high tech, so companies need an effective customer service department to answer the customer's enquiries and respond to any problems.

6. Production Knowledge Area

The production knowledge area covers the procurement, manufacture and distribution of the product. Many entrepreneurial projects start with making a prototype to test the product's performance and to confirm it can be built. This obviously relates to the technical content and scope of the new venture. It must be stressed that if the entrepreneur cannot produce a quality product that meets the clients needs, is competitive, reliable, and professionally supported by a willing

customer service, then the whole entrepreneurial endeavour will be self-limited.

Procurement: Procurement is the buying-in of goods and services to manufacture the product and run the company. Procurement might also include outsourcing of work.

Outsourcing (Chapter 11): Look on the back of any product you have bought recently and you will almost certainly see that it is made offshore, probably in China. Outsourcing and offshoring of work is increasing due to the cost differentials, particularly labour costs, which are significantly less in the East compared to the West (America and Europe).

Distribution (Chapter 12): Distribution is the process of moving a product within the supply chain. This includes distribution channels (hub and spoke), direct (Internet), transportation and warehousing.

7. Accounts Knowledge Area

The accounts knowledge area covers the financial aspects of running a small business which includes a number of plans and statements to manage the accounts.

Financial Statements (Chapter 13): This chapter summarises a number of financial statements the small business entrepreneur needs to be able to produce to manage the business and plan and control new ventures.

Business Plan (Chapter 14): As creative ideas and opportunities evolve into marketable products, at some point entrepreneurs need to formalise their approach with a coherent business plan. The business plan discusses the feasibility of pursuing the proposed venture and confirms it is making the best use of the entrepreneur's time and resources.

Sources of Finance *(Entrepreneurs Toolkit)*: Acquiring sufficient funding is a key component of any entrepreneurial venture. Without financial support and investment, innovative ideas and marketing opportunities cannot be developed, and may simply fall by the wayside as lost opportunities just waiting for another entrepreneur to pursue. Most entrepreneurial ventures need some form of financial support to oil the wheels of development.

Estimating (Chapter 15): For small business entrepreneurs to plan and control their work effectively, accurate estimating is essential. If you tender for work, then accurate estimating is even more important, because now you will be committing your business contractually, based on the estimate.

Cashflow (Chapter 16): The financial success of a new venture depends not only on the product making a profit, but also being able to finance the business through the start up and survival phases. Statistics clearly indicate that more companies go into liquidation because of cashflow problems than for any other reason. The small business entrepreneur must therefore closely plan and control the business' cashflow.

Breakeven Point (Chapter 17): The breakeven point analysis and the payback period are two important financial calculations which give the entrepreneur a feel for the venture's exposure to risk and uncertainty. The breakeven point calculates the number of units the company must sell to cover the set up costs (also called sunk costs), and the payback period calculates the time it will take to get there.

Cash Book (Chapter 18): The cash book method captures all the financial transactions within the company and logs them in a structured data base - it is from this data base that all the other accounting documents draw their raw data.

Red Tape (Chapter 19): Small business associations always complain about the amount of unnecessary red tape and the associated compliance costs which are disproportionately more onerous for the smaller businesses.

8. Small Business Management Techniques

The small business management techniques knowledge area covers all the key business management techniques entrepreneurs need in their portfolio of skills to manage a typical small business.

Entrepreneur: The small business entrepreneur and the small business manager are often thought of as being one and the same person. In some cases they are, but more often they are not. To distinguish between the two, it is important to clarify that entrepreneurship is essentially the management of change, particularly starting a new venture or introducing a new product or service. Whereas small business management is the management of the business on a day-to-day basis.

Entrepreneurship and small business management obviously go hand-in-hand. Small businesses swing in and out of periods of entrepreneurial change as the business introduces new products then consolidates its gains, before repeating the cycle at the next opportunity. For example, entrepreneurial change would include; the start up of the new business, the development of new products, the introduction of new management systems and the penetration of new markets. But, after each entrepreneurial change, the small business would typically consolidate the change and continue at the new level until there was a new need or opportunity to change again. This is shown graphically in figure 1.3.

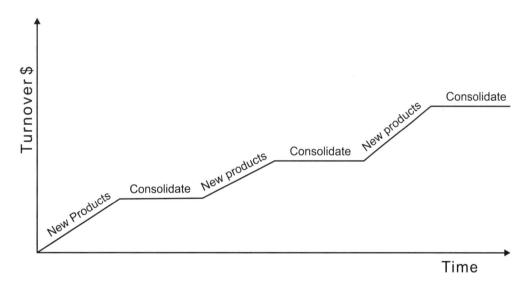

Figure 1.3: Entrepreneur / Small Business Manager Cycles - showing periods of entrepreneurship followed by periods of consolidation

Project Management: Setting up a new venture has all the characteristics of a small project which requires effective project management skills to plan and control the entrepreneurial process. For this reason project management is a core subject within entrepreneurship.

Team Building: The small business entrepreneur is the driving force behind new ventures - leading, co-ordinating, managing and organising the input of suppliers, contractors and team members.

Risk Management: Developing new ideas, seizing opportunities and starting new ventures will always involve an element of risk and uncertainty, and things inevitably will go wrong from time to time. Although entrepreneurs are usually stereotyped as foolhardy risk takers, how they manage their risks goes right to the heart of entrepreneurship.

9. Advantages of Setting up a Small Business

The small business environment is highly competitive and ruthless. This is supported by the statistics of small business survival which are not encouraging - up to 50% of start up businesses will cease trading within the first three years. It is therefore important to consider the pros and cons before embarking on this crusade so that you are aware of the risks and opportunities and can make an informed decision. Some of the advantages of setting up a small business are:

- you can be your own boss, work independently and increase the level of control you have on your life
- you can develop your hobbies and interests into a small business
- you will feel a great sense of achievement and receive recognition of your good work
- running a small business will give you the freedom and resources to pursue marketable opportunities
- you will be able to maximise the return of your financial investment
- you have a greater opportunity to make more money compared to earning a salary (see the chapter on *Staircase to Wealth*)
- you can increase your income security by offering a range of products to a wide client base (it is best not to have all your eggs in one basket)
- for the 50 plus, owning a small business enables them to overcome the age employment block and continue working
- although 50% of small businesses cease trading within three years, many of these companies cease for legitimate reasons which might have been as simple as a name change, moving to a different location, selling the business, or merging with another company.

10. Disadvantages of Setting up a Small Business

The exciting thoughts of setting up your own company could soon turn into a nightmare if you blindly march into a new venture. Consider the following disadvantages;

- your new venture and business could fail and you could lose all your investment, as well as any investment from your family and friends who you have persuaded to invest in your hare-brained scheme

- working long hours (24/7) may leave little time for your family and friends, and no time to live a life and pursue your hobbies and interests

- irregular supply of work will lead to uncertain income. In this feast or famine situation it is difficult to budget ahead

- you will be working on a tight budget as you try to cut costs while you are building up stock and business contacts. It could take a few years before you reach the breakeven point and positive cashflow kicks in

- working long hours with little time for relaxation and holidays increases your stress levels and could have a detrimental impact on your health

- you will be continually under pressure solving problems and making business decisions that you need to get right as your assets are on the line

- as you start your own business you will have to perform every job - from being the boss to cleaning up.

Setting up your own business is a major decision and commitment of your time and resources. Although the statistics of small business survival are a concern, the reason for failure is usually due to poor business management skills. But, as this Entrepreneurship Series shows, these small business management skills and techniques can be learnt.

Exercises:

1. The size of a SME is based on the number of employees and turnover - relate this to your business and the businesses you are familiar with.

2. Small businesses claim to be a big producer of new jobs. How has your business created new positions?

3. List the advantages of setting up your own small business.

Instructor's Manual: An Instructor's Manual is available with additional exercises and case studies, see *<www.knowledgezone.net>*.

2
Staircase to Wealth

"Who wants to be a millionaire?" is a popular TV programme which catches our imagination. We clearly associate wealth with happiness. More wealth equals more happiness. Wealth is perceived as giving us a big house, a quality car, holidays in the sun and no financial worries. The challenge is to acquire sufficient wealth to enjoy these pleasures in life.

The staircase to wealth gives an interesting step-by-step view of how to achieve the wealth we desire by looking at how we organise our business and develop our product, rather than pursuing an occupation. The staircase to wealth outlines how each step is primarily a learning experience (technical, managerial, business and entrepreneurial), preparing the entrepreneur for the next level. The staircase also outlines the potential product opportunities and financial risks at each level.

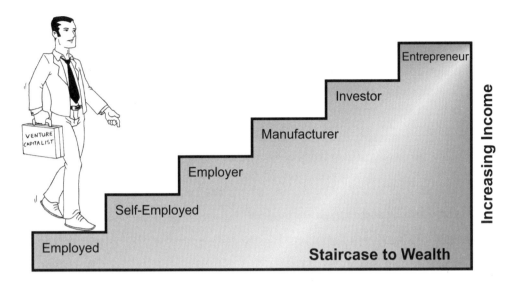

Figure 2.1 Staircase to Wealth

Figure 2.1 graphically portrays the staircase to wealth. Starting at the bottom of the stairs, people working for a salary (step 1) or self-employed people (step 2) cannot earn more than their labour rate, they can only gain leverage from education, promotion and working more hours.

However, employers (step 3) step up the staircase because they can gain leverage by earning a share of their employees' labour rate - the more employees, the more income.

Manufacturers are on the next step up (step 4) because they can gain leverage by earning a percentage mark-up on their products - the more products they sell, the more income.

Investors are on the next step up (step 5) because they can gain leverage by investing in rapid growth ventures - the greater the growth the greater the investor's profit.

Entrepreneurs are at the top of the staircase (step 6) because they are able to spot the marketable opportunity for a product in the first place . They are the market maker, making the link between the product and the market. They also make the venture happen, co-ordinating and managing all the stakeholders (investors, suppliers, manufacturers, distributors and retailers).

1. Employee (Step 1)

The bottom step of the staircase to wealth is the starting point for the career's of most people. With no work experience, no qualifications, no capital and no idea how to run a business - this is where most individuals would normally start serving their apprenticeship.

Once their training is completed, employed people gain leverage by being promoted up the corporate ladder, but their income is always going to be limited to their salary which is a function of their labour rate. However, at this point wealth creation is not necessarily where the focus should be - this is the time to develop technical and management skills.

Technical Skills: Every profession has its unique range of technical skills and as an apprentice you will be shown the ropes and learn '*the trade*'. Training courses will help you '*fast track*' up the learning curve. This is the opportunity to get a broad based grounding in all the technical aspects of the work, and acquire plenty of relevant work experience.

Management Skills: As an apprentice you will initially be given instructions on what to do and how to do it, and will be reporting to a supervisor. With increased technical competency, you will be given responsibility for your own work and eventually responsibility for managing a small team of workers who will report to you.

Business Skills: As a manager you are encouraged to make management and business decisions on a day-to-day basis. These decisions are usually based on risk management - on the fear of what could go wrong - rather than the entrepreneurial vision of new market opportunities and what could go right. It is this fear of making a mistake and the desire for security that stops many managers making the leap up the staircase to wealth, to the self-employment level.

Income: As an employee you generally work for a regular and secure monthly salary with statutory holiday pay, sickness benefit and a pension. Depending on the type of work and your position in the company, your income may be supplemented with such perks as a company car, business allowance, incentive bonus and even share options. With a predictable monthly income and expenses, this will ease you into managing your personal cashflow.

Tax: As an employed person there is limited opportunity to write off any expenses. The tax department expects that all direct business expenses will be refunded by the company you are working for, and the company itself will claim the expenses against their income.

Salaried managers often give the illusion of wealth because, apart from the impressive job title (General Manager or CEO), the position includes a plush office, personal assistant, company car, business lunches, business accommodation, and business class travel; but this could be a gilded cage as all these luxuries are linked to the job. When the manager retires or is made redundant all these business perks will be lost along with the job.

Entrepreneur Skills: There are three basic reasons why an entrepreneur would seek an employed position:

- to learn a specific skill in a field he wants to enter
- to obtain a trade licence
- to build-up capital to fund a new venture.

If you want to set up a new venture in a field you are not familiar with, then seeking employment in that field is a sensible way to quickly learn the ropes. For example, if you want to open a restaurant, then first find a job in a restaurant to learn all the different jobs from peeling potatoes to serving the patrons. The owner of the restaurant may even be prepared to mentor your new business.

Certain positions require a special licence. For example, if you want to set up a freight business, you could take a job with a trucking company, learn the trade and get a HGV (Heavy Goods Vehicle) driving licence at the same time.

The third reason an entrepreneur might seek employment is to build-up capital to invest in a new venture. Start up companies are usually financed by personal funds or funds from family and friends. The other sources of finance, banks, business angels and venture capital firms, usually prefer to invest in established companies.

To be successful entrepreneurs must be able to spot opportunities and be proficient in their line of work. Both of these attributes are developed through work experience. This is supported by the fact that 80% of entrepreneurs start their first business in the same field in which they have been working.

One of the reasons often cited for entrepreneurs leaving a large company and starting their own business is lack of support and enthusiasm for their innovative and creative ideas. This ultimately leads to frustration and the search for something more enterprising.

2. Self-Employment (Step 2)

It is a brave decision to jump from full-time employment in an established company to insecure self-employment with unknown work prospects and unpredictable income and cashflow. But taking this step will increase the entrepreneur's labour rate and fast track the learning of technical, managerial, business and entrepreneurial skills.

Taking this first step into self-employment says a lot about the entrepreneur's level of self-confidence and ability to go out there and do it. And as a self-employed person, the entrepreneur will be able to gain leverage on the charge out labour rate.

Technical Skills: As a self-employed contractor you could be performing exactly the same work that you were performing before as an employee, but now you will be perceived as an expert in your particular trade or profession.

However, when there is a downturn in the business cycle or economy, as a self-employed contractor, you will probably be the first person to be laid-off, because full-time employees have secure employment. The benefit of this situation is that it will encourage you as an entrepreneur to become a *jack of all trades* to ensure a wide range of continuous employment. This is good training for a future management role where you will acquire a broad range of technical skills and work experience.

Management Skills: As a self-employed person you will need to quickly learn how to run a small business. Besides the technical side of the work, you will have to manage the accounts, invoicing, payroll, procurement, cashflow, estimating, book keeping, budgets and taxation.

As a self-employed person you will not be able to pass the buck as easily as an employee can; the buck stops with the self-employed contractor who must ultimately be responsible professionally and financially for the standard of work.

Business Skills: As a self-employed contractor working in a competitive market you will need to spend more time networking and marketing to secure ongoing employment. This involves networking with potential clients, promoting and advertising your products, cold calling, and making presentations to potential buyers and clients. This is excellent training for the next step up the ladder.

One of the problems with self-employment is that you spend half your time marketing (trying to find work), half your time doing the work and half your time doing the accounts and chasing payments!!!

With an uncertain supply of work, you may feel obliged to bid on a variety of projects outside your core competencies. This will help develop the entrepreneurial trait of spotting new business opportunities, plus forming alliances with other sub-contractors in order to share work and risks.

".... I spend half my time marketing, half my time working, and half my time doing the accounts....!?"

Income: As a self-employed contractor you will have a different contractual relationship with your client, even though you may be doing exactly the same work as you were doing before as an employee. You should earn more on an hourly rate compared to a salaried employee, but you need to balance this with no sick leave protection, no holiday pay, less job security, and unproductive (earning) time spent marketing and doing the accounts. This could mean you are only earning an income part of the time. With uncertain and irregular income the control of your cashflow becomes increasingly more difficult and financially more important.

Tax: As a self-employed contractor you will need to register yourself as a sole trader, partnership, or limited company. These types of business structures are able to claim for a wide range of business expenses and VAT. And further, you only pay income tax on the profits.

Entrepreneur Skills: Self-employment enables entrepreneurs to develop networking, sales and marketing skills. If entrepreneurs can generate more work than they can do themselves, this is the opportunity for them to expand and become an employer.

3. Employer (Step 3)

As an employer the entrepreneur moves up the staircase to wealth and can now gain leverage by earning a percentage of the employees' charge out labour rate - the more employees the more income. This section focuses on the management of people while the following section focuses on manufacturing the product and its supply chain.

Technical Skills: As an employer you will probably start working close to the 'coalface' but, as the business grows you need to learn how to delegate the technical work in order to free up your own time, and also to allow the employees to take responsibility for their own work.

The strength of a business lies with the empowerment of its workers and the people managing them. As **Henry Ford** said, ".... *it is important to employ people who are smarter than you in every field of your business....*". This helps to not only overcome your shortcomings, but also stop you trying to do all the jobs yourself - why would you if you have a team of experts?

Management Skills: As the business grows so the company needs to expand its workforce. This is good HR (Human Resource) training for the entrepreneur in recruitment, team building, leadership and communication.

The **team** structure outlines the relationship between the team leader (entrepreneur) and the other team members. The recruitment and selection of team members must address both the technical skills required and balance the team roles. The membership of the team may be dynamic and transitional as people move in and out of the new venture.

Without dynamic **leadership**, the project team would be like a rudderless boat. You need strong leadership skills to solve problems, make decisions and give the team direction.

New ventures are run by **communication**. As the business grows communication is one of the first management systems to come under pressure. This pressure is good training for the entrepreneur to establish a more formal communication system which strikes a balance between the entrepreneur's naturally casual way of communication, which has worked well in the past, and a more structured communication system with scheduled meetings and documentation control.

As an entrepreneur you will need to develop **team building** and **leadership** skills which enable you to:
- delegate through a climate of trust
- design and implement business systems to process and communicate information and instructions

- build relationships with stakeholders, particularly clients, contractors, suppliers, distributors and retailers
- solve-problems and make decisions quickly and effectively.

Business Skills: With an increasing workforce you will need to develop an effective sales and marketing team to keep the jobs flowing in and the workforce gainfully employed. With all aspects of the business growing (investment, work force, wage bill and sales), this will be good training in managing a fluctuating cashflow.

Income: As an employer you will earn a share of the employees' charge out labour rate. The labour rate is typically split into thirds to cover the following expenses;

- 1/3 to cover the employee's salary and associated costs
- 1/3 to cover supervision and company overheads
- 1/3 to repay debts and company profit.

It is therefore obvious that the more workers the business employs the more profit you should make. That is assuming you can keep all the employees working on charge out jobs. You will, however, need to be continually monitoring the ratio of worked hours to charge out hours.

Tax: As the owner of a business you will need to register the business as a sole trader, partnership, or limited company - probably the latter. All these types of businesses are able to claim for business expenses and VAT reclaim, and only pay income tax on the profits.

Entrepreneur Skills: Managing a growing business will give the entrepreneur the opportunity to learn how to design and develop a team structure and company organisation structure. To go forward, the business needs an effective management team and a company organisation structure it can rely on.

As the business develops integrated management systems and the entrepreneur's approach changes to a more formal management style, so the entrepreneur will learn to value the benefits of delegation, empowerment and employing experts. The entrepreneur will also see that these management systems can be applied to improving manufacturing efficiency and integrating the supply chain.

4. Manufacturer (Step 4)

As the owner of a manufacturing business the entrepreneur moves up the staircase to wealth and can now gain leverage by earning a percentage mark-up on each product the company sells. The more products the company sells, the more income.

While the previous section focused on the management of people within the business, this section focuses on the efficient manufacturing of the product to lower the unit costs, together with ways the business can expand within its supply chain.

Technical Skills: As the owner of a growing manufacturing company, you will spend less time on technical issues and more time on production management and managing the supply chain.

Management Skills: Managing a rapid growth company is the entrepreneur's Achilles' heel because increased sales can lead to a company **success-disaster** situation. A success-disaster can happen when the sales and marketing team hits the sweet spot and demand for the product suddenly takes off. If your knee-jerk reaction is to try and gear up production to meet the demand this could lead to a disaster if the manufacturing, distribution and finance cannot keep up. The increased demand could create supply shortages, stressed out workers and negative cashflow which could ultimately lead to liquidation.

Product shortages could cause the help desk to get swamped with enquiries from angry customers. The knock-on impact of the inability to deliver could result in the business developing a bad reputation with its customers, and this could allow your competitors into the very market you have pioneered and developed.

While your business is small, you can manage everything in your head on a day-to-day basis. But with rapid growth, your ad hoc management style needs to change to a more formalised management approach to enable effective planning and control. And herein lies the problem; entrepreneurs, by their very nature, are motivated by opportunities, freedom, risk and profit, whereas managers are motivated by resources, delegation and security.

This is an excellent opportunity for you to learn the techniques of **supply chain management**. All companies sit somewhere in a supply chain, between suppliers and clients. You will learn how to trade-off just-in-time (JIT) supply with material stock and the risk of production down time. You will also learn the trade-off between long production runs to reduce the unit cost, with increased warehousing and inventory costs.

As new product designs stabilise and the customer base grows, so manufacturing companies gain leverage through productivity by investing in automated manufacturing facilities to reduce the unit cost. This gives the company the potential to increase the market share, increase the profit margin, and ultimately increase the return on investment.

For example, a small boat building company making a number of yachts of different designs might see a market for mass producing one particular design. By investing in production line facilities, they should be able to greatly increase their output and slash their unit costs. Increasing the level of capital expenditure per employee should improve the productivity rate.

Business Skills: With large capital investments in manufacturing equipment, the sales and marketing team have an increasing number of mouths to feed with work. This is a good time for the entrepreneur to learn sales and marketing skills.

As a small business you might be mass producing components for a number of large companies that then assemble the components into a marketable product. These large companies are effectively outsourcing part of their work to you. This is good training for the entrepreneur looking for horizontal and vertical expansion within the supply chain.

Income: The manufacturing process incurs significant up-front costs (design, manufacturing set up, stocking and distribution, together with marketing, advertising and promotion). These up-front costs will have a negative impact on the cashflow until the income from the product's sales reaches its breakeven point. See the chapter on *Breakeven Point* for details on how to calculate the breakeven point and the payback period.

Entrepreneur Skills: As the company moves into large scale production and the entrepreneur survives the success-disaster scenario, so the entrepreneur will learn to value the benefits of delegation, empowerment and employing experts. The entrepreneur will also see the important role investors play in the business cycle and how the investors stand to earn the lions' share from company growth. This will encourage the entrepreneur to look for potential growth prospects outside the company.

5. Investor (Step 5)

Investors lubricate the wheels of industry and commerce. All businesses need financial support from time to time, particularly during the start up and the rapid growth phases. As an investor, the entrepreneur moves up the staircase to wealth and can now gain leverage by investing in rapid growth businesses - the greater the growth, the greater the return on investment.

It should be acknowledged that of all the businesses that register each year only 5% of them can be considered as rapid growth businesses. Therefore, the entrepreneur investor will need to select the businesses to invest in with due diligence.

Technical Skills: Investors use their technical knowledge to ensure the businesses they invest in have the manufacturing equipment and technical expertise to achieve production targets.

Management Skills: Investors use their management knowledge to ensure the businesses they invest in have the production management systems and production management expertise to manage the manufacturing facility effectively and efficiently.

Business Skills: Investors use their business knowledge to ensure the businesses they invest in have the business and marketing skills to open new markets to keep the orders flowing in. There are two types of commercial investors - business angels and venture capital firms. Business angels often help businesses by mentoring the manager(s), while venture capital firms might want a seat on the board to monitor the business at the operational level, and have a say in business strategy.

Business Angels' Skills: Business angels are usually wealthy private investors who are willing to provide small amounts of their own capital to seed entrepreneurial ventures, unlike the institutional venture capital firms, which invest other people's money. Business angels not only bring an injection of funds into a venture, but also a wealth of entrepreneurial experience and contacts which may be invaluable for a fledgling start up.

Typically, business angels bring a lot more than just cash to the venture and will offer advice and experience to help refine the business over time. In many cases, early stage businesses require less equity (funds) than many venture capital firms are willing to invest, which leaves it up to the business angels to fill this funding void.

Venture Capitalists' Skills: Venture capital firms professionally manage a pool of equity capital. The equity pool is usually formed from the resources of wealthy partners, pension funds, endowment funds, large corporations and other institutions. The pool is managed by a venture capital firm in exchange for a percentage of the investment.

As a result, the venture capital firms tend to have deeper pockets than other investors but they also have obligations to their investors and are, therefore, more circumspect about which businesses they invest in.

The purpose of venture capital firms is to generate long-term capital appreciation through debt and equity investments. Venture capital firms are therefore looking for entrepreneurial businesses with good rapid growth prospects.

Income: Both business angels and venture capital firms are not looking for short term income (dividends) because they know this cannot give them the high returns they require to offset their investment risks. They plan to make their return by rapidly growing the business and realising the capital gain through an exit strategy, by selling their equity stake to either another business or an IPO (Initial Public Offering) flotation on the stock market.

Entrepreneur Skills: Investment skills form an important part of the entrepreneurs' portfolio of management skills. It is one of their core competencies. Investment skills teach entrepreneurs the value of money in the business process. With technical, managerial and investment skills under their belt, entrepreneurs are well prepared to start entrepreneurial ventures of their own.

Level	Leverage
Employee	Apprenticeship, promotion
Self-employed	Labour rate
Employer	Number of employees
Manufacturer	Mass production
Investor	Return on investment from capital growth
Entrepreneur	Spot opportunities

Figure 2.2: Summary of Leverage Potential - this table summarizes the leverage potential as the entrepreneur progresses up the staircase to wealth

6. Entrepreneur (Step 6)

Entrepreneurs are experts at spotting opportunities and organising resources to make new ventures happen. They have the vision and business skills to spot an innovative and marketable opportunity, together with the self-confidence to make the decision to set up the new venture and the courage to accept the associated risks. And, once the venture has started, they have the drive and leadership qualities to overcome any problems to make-it-happen.

As an entrepreneur, you are at the top of the staircase to wealth because you are the key person at the heart of a new venture. As an entrepreneur you gain leverage by being the market maker - you get the ball rolling. You spot the opportunity, you start up the new venture, you organise the resources, you manage and co-ordinate the input of the key players and stakeholders, and you sell the product to the customers.

Entrepreneur Traits: Entrepreneurs have a number of traits and behaviours which distinguish them from lesser business mortals. These traits combine in different ways to give the entrepreneur their ad hoc management style and that special X factor, which enables them to do the unexpected - successfully. Although entrepreneurs have a number of similar traits they do not fit into any one particular mould - every one of them is different.

Spot Opportunities: Entrepreneurs are experts at spotting the opportunities other people only see in hindsight. They use a combination of creative thinking, innovation, lateral thinking and instinct to find simple marketable opportunities.

Internal Locus of Control: Entrepreneurs with a strong internal locus of control believe their lives, their destiny and their successes are determined by their own actions and not by the actions of others. If they fail, they accept that it is because of their own actions. So, by analysing their actions and addressing their shortcomings, entrepreneurs believe they will be successful next time round.

Self-Confidence: Entrepreneurs believe in themselves. They are self-confident and know they can do the job and this is reflected in their decision-making. Research shows that entrepreneurs are statistically more **confident** of their decisions than other managers, even though the entrepreneurs' decisions are no better than other managers and, in many cases, are actually wrong.

Passion: Entrepreneurs have a passion for their product and a tenacity to keep trying again and again until they get it right, long after most people would have given up and moved on.

Decision-Making: A large number of entrepreneurs have had a difficult childhood, did poorly at school and are further 'handicapped' by being dyslexic. One would have thought this would set them back, but experts believe that because dyslexics have difficulty understanding the details, they excel by grasping the bigger picture. They do not waste time analysing the detail and are therefore able to make decisions much more quickly.

Determination: Entrepreneurs are highly competitive. They will do whatever it takes to get their product to market first. They will cut corners to by-pass unnecessary bureaucratic rules and regulations, and work all hours of the day and night to fast track their product to completion. Why? Because they instinctively know that the first to market catches the lions' share of the customers and also gets a better price for their product. Entrepreneurs are able to totally focus all their energies (110%) into making their product a success.

Networking: Networking is one of the key traits of entrepreneurs enabling them to gain access to useful information and the free use of resources - this helps to enhance the entrepreneur's competitive advantage.

Optimistic: Entrepreneurs are hugely optimistic, full of energy and extremely exciting to be around, but they are also stubborn, single-minded and selfish.

Risk Traits: Entrepreneurs are usually stereotyped as foolhardy risk takers, almost by definition, marching into new ventures where *angels fear to tread*. To understand how entrepreneurs deal with risk, failure and rejection goes right to the heart of entrepreneurship. Although the management techniques provide a structured methodology for entrepreneurs to follow, to really understand their approach to risk, failure and rejection one has to look at their personal traits, notably internal locus of control, self-confidence, optimism and courage.

Project Management: Setting up a new venture has all the characteristics of a small project which requires effective project management skills to plan and control the entrepreneurial process. Entrepreneurs intuitively use project management techniques to co-ordinate and manage the input of the stakeholders (clients, investors, suppliers, manufacturers and distributors). Entrepreneurs have a multitude of challenges to face when implementing new ventures so it is important to ensure innovative ideas and opportunities are not handicapped at the outset by ineffective project management.

7. Step Down The Staircase

Would you believe some people might actually prefer to step down the staircase! Yes, actually want to earn less money!

After working as a self-employed person or running your own business you may decide that it is all too much like hard work and you long for the good old days of secure employment. There are a number of advantages in returning to full-time employment. Consider the following points:

- full-time employment offers a sense of job security
- you receive a regular pay cheque, annual holiday pay, sickness benefit and a pension - all these make it easier to plan your life and manage your finances. Even though you may earn less income, at least your salary is regular
- you work normal hours, have weekends off, can go on planned holidays with your family and see your children grow - basically you live a normal life
- you are able to take sick leave when you are ill and not have to worry about the business collapsing while you recover in bed
- you have lower stress levels - instead of worrying about your risky investments you worry about your golf swing
- you want to specialise in your profession and work in an environment which has the latest facilities - this particularly applies to companies working on leading edge and high tech products. It is only large companies and government institutions that can offer these facilities
- you want to be part of a team, rather than working on your own, because team membership offers a number of benefits and psychological support
- a large company or institution usually offers better access to training courses and personal development, and has the budget to send you to professional conferences and trade exhibitions around the world
- you may wish to work solely in your area of expertise and not be involved in other areas you feel uncomfortable with. For example, many technical engineers do not want to be part of the sales and marketing team - they prefer to focus solely on their research or product
- many technical people do not like handling money. They do not like sending out invoices and particularly do not like chasing up bad debts from clients who are slow payers.

As a team, your colleagues are always there to provide technical advice and help solve your problems. Interactive teams generate a cross-flow of new creative ideas and, through team synergy, the team may actually produce better ideas collectively than they would individually. Team members provide a good sounding board to test ideas, encouraging and motivating you to perform - you do not want to let the side down.

Entrepreneurship and small business management is not the panacea for everyone. There are many professionals and academics who prefer to work for large companies, international institutions or governments that are able to provide the infrastructure and technical support they need to pursue their professions.

Exercises:

1. Where are you on the staircase to wealth? How did you get there and what are your plans for the future?

2. To earn $1m per year profit, calculate your labour rate as a self-employed contractor.

3. Do you know anyone who has gone back into full-time employment after running their own business? Discuss their rationale.

Instructor's Manual: An Instructor's Manual is available with additional exercises and case studies, see <www.knowledgezone.net>.

3
What Type of Work?

Deciding to start your own business is a brave decision, particularly if you have to give up a well paid secure job. But, this is only the beginning - the next brave decision is to decide on what type of work to do or what type of product to sell. This is where you need to combine the skills of an entrepreneur to spot a marketable opportunity with the skills of a small business manager to run a business on a day-to-day basis.

There is a general misconception that to start a new business you have to offer something completely new and original, something earth shatteringly complicated and high tech that no one has thought of before. But, entrepreneurs have always known that the secret is to find a simple way of providing something that is perceived to be better, cheaper or more efficient than what is currently available. This could even be something that is exactly the same as another product but is not available locally (franchising uses this approach).

Entrepreneurship can be presented as a logical sequence of inter-related management topics (opportunities, marketing, sources of finance and production), which are linked through an iterative spiral. By repeating the loop of the spiral many times each management topic can be developed progressively to converge on an optimum solution.

A new product will only be successful if the small business entrepreneur can make the link between the new product and the market because, even with the best product in the world, if it does not have a market it will not be successful. Conversely, an ordinary product which has an enthusiastic market will do well.

Other key items to consider are how you plan to finance the small business, how you plan to manufacture the product, and how you plan to distribute the product to the customers.

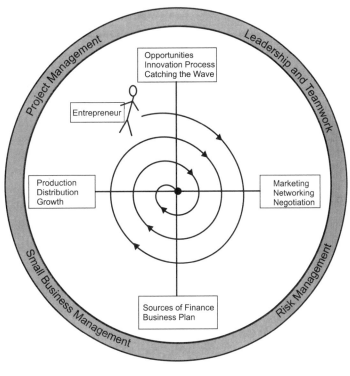

Figure 3.1: Entrepreneurial Spiral from *Entrepreneurs Toolkit*

1. Stay in Your Trade

Statistically 80% of entrepreneurs start their first business in their field of expertise - the same field they have been working in for most of their career. Although this may not sound very entrepreneurial, it is a natural approach because it avoids having to learn a new trade at the same time as learning to run a small business. Entrepreneurs are also more likely to spot opportunities in their own field of expertise and, further, know how to implement them.

For instance, if you are a qualified plumber, electrician or carpenter, then you could consider setting up a small business offering your services locally. If there is already a business offering the same service, then you could consider targeting the neighbouring areas.

2. Lateral Thinking

If there is local competition in your trade, profession or product, think laterally about other products you could offer which are linked to your expertise. For example, if you are a plumber, instead of offering plumbing services directly to customers consider;

- opening a plumbing hardware shop to sell bathroom and kitchen fittings
- setting up a factory to manufacture plumbing components
- setting up training courses for the home builder
- writing training manuals on plumbing.

Small business entrepreneurs are experts at getting around blocks, and turning problems into opportunities. And, if they can move their business up the staircase to wealth, they will probably do financially better in the long run.

3. Lifestyle Hobby

An increasing number of people are trying to strike a balance between earning mega-bucks in the city and having a meaningful lifestyle, perhaps in the country. They feel that earning a large salary is not an end in itself and are looking for a more balanced lifestyle. These people are using their entrepreneurial skills to set up lifestyle businesses, particularly turning their hobby and interests into a business - for example:

- a person who enjoys golf opens a golf pro shop
- a person who enjoys cooking opens a restaurant
- a person who enjoys fashion opens a boutique

- a person who enjoys working on cars opens a garage
- a person who enjoys watching films opens a DVD hire shop
- a person who enjoys working on computers designs web sites.

Pursuing a hobby can be a double edged sword. On the one hand, your passion will get you through the long hours, and your skills will help to solve technical problems, but on the other hand, your love for the hobby may blind you from its commercial reality and, once you have sunk a lot of money into a white elephant, it may be too late to change direction.

4. Solve a Problem

Anita Roddick (Body Shop) said, "*If you ever sense a problem, you have just found another opportunity*". Turning a problem into a marketable product is a key entrepreneurial trait. For instance, Richard Branson solved the problem of supplying cheap music to students by selling them second hand LPs by mail order at knock down prices (see the chapter on *Working From Home* for more information), and Steve Jobs solved a similar problem more recently by offering cheap music downloads to the Apple ipod.

Another famous example of turning a problem into an opportunity happened to Howard Hughes (senior), who was forced to abandon an oil well because he could not drill though a layer of rock (technology block). He then founded Hughes Tool Co. and invented a rock drill to solve the problem. This developed to become the foundation for the family fortune.

Computer technology is often thought of as '*... a solution looking for a problem*'. For example, the spreadsheet is a mathematical matrix which has many numerical applications - the entrepreneurial accountants were quick to spot its usefulness for managing companies' accounts.

5. Buying a Business

Why go to all the trouble of setting up a business when you can buy an established business off the shelf? Buying a ready made business means the business will already have an established product and client base - if the cap fits you will at least hit the ground running. All you need to do is jump in the hot seat and take over the controls (see the chapter on *Buying a Business* for more information).

6. Buying a Franchise

Why go to all the trouble of searching for a business concept when you can buy into an established franchise business. Yes - buying into a franchise business has become a popular way of starting a business. This is encouragingly supported by the statistics that show that a franchise business is more likely to be successful than an independent start up business - it is definitely worth considering (see the chapter on *Buying a Franchise* for more information).

7. Types of Business

Another way of looking at what type of work to pursue is to consider the four main types of business activities:
- Manufacturing and construction
- Distribution
- Retail
- Services

Manufacturing and Construction: Manufacturing and construction is all about co-ordinating resources (materials, components and labour), and managing work interfaces. You will need technical expertise and should be prepared to work long hours and perhaps work shifts. Manufacturing and construction will require large injections of capital to buy machinery and materials which will have a negative impact on the cashflow. However, there is the reward of having created a useful product.

Distribution: As a distributor you are essentially the middleman in the supply chain operating between the manufacturer and the customer. Distribution includes importing, wholesaling, warehousing and transporting products. Success in this area comes from having excellent buying and selling skills. Distribution businesses are generally low in staffing requirements, have good cashflows and often involve constant travel to keep in-touch with customers and suppliers.

Retail: Retailers are the last link in the supply chain supplying products to the end customers. Retailers use a variety of advertising and promotions to attract customers to their stores (this includes mail order and buying online). If you like dealing with people (customers), then this type of work could be right for you. Retailing is all about selling products to people. It should generate good cashflows, but can be unpredictable due to buyer behaviours (fads) and seasonal markets (fashion seasons).

Services: This is probably the most popular type of work for small businesses. Services are about working with people and providing them with your skills and expertise. A service type product could include; cleaning, accounting, computer maintenance, hosting web sites, and consultancy.

The service industry relies on the selling of time and skills. To work in this field you need to enjoy working with customers and providing a service. You will need to be efficient at managing resources and at maximising charge out time - this will be the key to your profitability. Most service businesses do not need vast amounts of cash to get started as they do not usually require specialist equipment or large quantities of stock. The business can grow to suit the market, from the owner operator to several staff. These types of business generally provide good cashflow.

Each type of work has its own unique characteristics that may or may not suit your skills, strengths and personality. If you enjoy working with people then maybe you should try providing a service or run a retail outlet. If you are happier working on your own then maybe you should try manufacturing a product in your garage. And if you enjoy travelling then maybe you should try marketing and distributing a product.

Business Plan: Whatever type of work you decide to explore, it is essential to evaluate the feasibility of your idea with a comprehensive business plan. The business plan should confirm the product can be made or provided, that there is a market for the product, and that you are making the best use of your resources (see the chapter on *Business Plans* for more information).

Exercises:

1. Present a commercial proposal to solve a problem that you have identified.

2. Discuss which of your hobbies or interests could be developed into a small business.

3. Use lateral thinking to show how someone with a basic trade or profession could use these skills to form a small business.

Instructor's Manual: An Instructor's Manual is available with additional exercises and case studies, see <www.knowledgezone.net>.

4
Registering A Small Business

When you set up a new business you need to establish a legal identity for the new enterprise to comply with statutory requirements. There are three main legal identities to consider;

- sole trader
- partnership
- limited company

Each of these types of businesses have different statutory requirements to comply with and offer different levels of legal protection. The entrepreneur needs to consider the pros and cons of each identity to determine which is the most appropriate structure for the proposed type of business.

It does not matter how great the product is, or how competitive the price, if you do not have a sound legal platform to drive the business you will be missing out on many of the advantages registration provides. But, of more concern, you will be setting yourself up for legal and financial battles ahead.

".... businesses come in all shapes and sizes ...."

1. Sole Trader

Setting up as a sole trader is the most common and simplest way of starting a small business. As the name suggests, the business is owned by one person. For the purposes of liability and income tax, the owner and the business are considered one and the same. Although the sole trader's personal property is not considered part of the business assets, if there are business debts, then personal property can be appropriated to pay the debts (so be warned).

Advantages of a Sole Trade: There are many advantages for the entrepreneur to register as a sole trader. Consider the following:

- the biggest advantage of this type of business is that it is simple to set up and simple to run. It is also the least expensive and quickest business structure to get started
- as the owner, you are in complete control of the business and do not have to report to anyone - at last you are your own boss!
- as the boss you are top of the pecking order which, research has shown, actually reduces stress because you are only making decisions for yourself and not having to second guess for your boss

- as an entrepreneur, you can develop your own ideas in your own way without having to answer to anybody else - doing it '*my way*' gives enormous personal satisfaction
- you keep all the business profit as there are no other shareholders
- you decide where the income goes - into your pocket or reinvested to give sustainable growth
- apart from tax returns, a sole trader is not required to make public any information about the business
- the sole trader structure has the least amount of red tape and therefore the least amount of compliance costs
- a sole trader operation can be dissolved as simply and as quickly as it was set up.

Operating your business as a sole trader has many advantages, mainly because you are able to give a personal service to your customers and are able to make changes within your business very quickly. Other advantages include having complete control over the business and its profits; you are able to use the profits as you deem fit without having to justify your spending - so remember these facts and exploit them.

Disadvantages of a Sole Trader: As a sole trader, the entrepreneur is in a very vulnerable and exposed position. Consider the following points;

- you have to accept unlimited liability for all business debts and legal claims against your business
- your personal possessions such as the car, house and furniture can be seized to pay any business debts
- if your business fails you have no protection - all your assets become available to pay off the creditors
- if you do not have a track record as a sole trader you might have difficulty acquiring funds. This means you will have to provide most of the capital yourself from personal funds which could limit the business' growth potential and, consequently, let the competitors expand into '*your*' market
- registering as a sole trader does not offer you the same protection for your trading name as registering as a limited company.

The key to success is to exploit the advantages of being a sole trader and try and mitigate the disadvantages. As the enterprise develops, the entrepreneur needs to consider the future business options. There could be a good business case for taking on a partner(s) to widen the expertise base, share the workload and share the investment.

2. Partnership

A partnership is a legal agreement between two or more people to work together. If two or more people work together in a business and no one is an '*employee*' then the law regards the arrangement as a partnership. The earnings are distributed according to the partnership agreement and then treated as personal income for tax purposes.

Advantages of a Partnership: There are many advantages for the entrepreneur to set up as a partnership. Consider the following:

- forming a partnership basically has the same advantages as becoming a sole trader with the added advantage of interactive team work
- a partnership is easier and less expensive to establish than a limited company
- the more partners, the more sources of finance
- the more partners, the wider the range of complementary skills (see Rolls Royce example below)
- interaction between the partners can generate more creative ideas and synergy compared to working as individuals (remember what Lennon-McCartney achieved)
- the more partners there are, the wider the network of contacts
- partnerships benefit from team dynamics; moral support, technical support, encouragement and motivation
- the more hands there are to share the workload, the quicker the jobs will be completed, and the less need to employ workers from outside the company.

Disadvantages of a Partnership: A partnership can suffer from the same disadvantages as a sole trader business, plus a few of its own making. Consider the following:

- all the partners share the liability of the partnership (see below for discussion on partnership debts)
- unless there is an agreement to the contrary, the profits will be equally shared between the partners irrespective of who does the work
- even with a partnership agreement, the profits might be shared as per the share holding and not as per work input and earning ability
- there is more paperwork required in setting up the partnership agreement, compared to setting up as a sole trader, as each member is likely to bring issues to the table which must be discussed and agreed
- setting up a partnership agreement takes time and could be expensive

- with two or more people of equal status involved in the decision-making, the response time might be slower than a sole trader
- as the number of partners increases, so the potential for conflict increases.

Many of these disadvantages can be addressed directly by developing a well structured partnership agreement. It is recommended that a partnership agreement be arranged to legalise the partnership. This will help to avoid and clear up any disputes which may arise concerning profit, liabilities and responsibility.

Complementary Skills: One of the advantages of forming a partnership is that each partner can bring different complementary skills into the business - this might well be the reason for forming a partnership in the first place.

Many successful entrepreneurial companies have developed out of a partnership of two or more people with complementary skills. **Rolls Royce** is an excellent example of a partnership, where the combination of Henry Royce's engineering skills and Charles Rolls' sales and marketing skills produced high quality cars for the luxury market.

"... you build them - I'll sell them ..."

Partnership Agreement: In some respects partnerships are an accident waiting to happen. Without a certain amount of flexibility between the partners, the partnerships could easily fall into disagreement, conflict and disarray. However, some of the potential sources of conflict can be avoided by establishing a 'partnership agreement' at the outset. The partnership agreement should clarify and determine the following points:

- the capital contributions from each partner
- the payment ratio of each partner, particularly if it is not an equal split
- how the profits and losses will be allocated
- how the salaries will be related to the work done
- the liability of each partner, particularly if it is not an equal split
- the responsibility of each partner, the seniority and who has control over the business
- who plans and sets the vision
- who is responsible for sales and marketing the products
- who is responsible for manufacturing and distributing the products
- who is responsible for the accounts, invoices and payments
- who is in charge of customer service
- how a partner leaves the business
- the rules on admitting new partners
- how to end the partnership.

By confirming and clarifying all these details the partnership agreement establishes a sound platform on which the partnership can operate.

Partnership Debts: It may come as a surprise to discover that each partner is responsible for all the other partners' debts. Yes, this means if one of the partners builds up debts and does a runner the remaining partner(s) has to pick up the bill. This is because partners have a shared responsibility for repaying all the partnership's debts.

Accounting companies are usually sole traders or partnerships so, it was with some surprise to many to hear that when the **Arthur Andersen** accounting firm got into trouble over **Enron,** the 'partners' around the world were suddenly not 'partners' any more. This was obviously to avoid liability for the Enron fallout - talk about diving for cover.

To overcome the liability issue there are a number of hybrid arrangements which limit the partners' liability. One of the key features of a hybrid arrangement is to encourage outside investment without the liability.

3. Limited Company

A limited company, unlike a sole trader and a partnership is a legal identity in its own right. Its shareholders and directors may change, but the company continues to exist as a separate identity. A limited company, as the name suggests, limits the liabilities of the directors and shareholders should the company fail or be sued. In the worst case the shareholders' liability would be limited to their share capital.

Unless there is a special reason, small business owners do not usually start trading as a limited company because of the additional costs and requirements. It is much easier to start as a sole trader or a partnership.

Advantages of a Limited Company: There are a number of clear advantages of operating through a limited company:
- limited liability
- ease of raising funds
- credibility with customers and suppliers (stakeholders)
- name protection

Limited Liability: In a limited liability company each shareholder' liability is limited to the amount of money and assets he or she has put into the business (hence the term limited liability). As long as the shareholders and directors of a company have not done anything illegal or negligent, the shareholders of a limited liability company cannot be made to pay out of their own pockets for the debts of the company. No business liability can overlap on to their personal assets, because a limited liability company is viewed in legal terms as a separate entity in its own right.

Limited companies were designed to recognise that a person should be able to own shares in a company without having to accept all of the risks associated with the way the company operates in the marketplace.

Raising Capital: Unlike the sole trader and a partnership which must rely on the individuals' personal funds, a limited company can offer equity (ownership in the company) to outside investors. This enables a rapidly growing company to raise capital through a public offering of its stock.

Credibility: A limited company may be perceived by some stakeholders as a more stable and professional operation than the sole trader (one man band).

Name Protection: Registration of a limited liability company also protects the **business name** from being used by another company. Once a name is approved by the Registrar of Companies, no other company can be registered with the same or near-same name.

Disadvantages of a Limited Company: There are a number of disadvantages which should be considered:

- the limited liability protection may be overridden by investors requiring personal guarantees from the directors
- there are increased regulatory burdens and company audits
- shareholders dilute the entrepreneurs' share of the profits.

A limited company is more expensive to register than a sole trader or a partnership, but, in the West, the costs involved have reduced significantly in recent years. For a comparison of compliance requirements and ease of registration see the chapter on *Red Tape* for the Doing Business Database compiled by the World Bank.

	Advantages	Disadvantages
Sole Trader	Simple to set up and simple to operate	Owner has full liability
Partnership	Complementary skills	Each partner has full liability for all the partnership's debts
Limited Company	Limited liability	Increased regulatory burden

Figure 4.1: Summary of Company Types

Exercises:

1. Many entrepreneurs start as a sole trader - give some examples in your local area.

2. One of the key benefits of a partnership is the positive interaction between the members - give an example.

3. Governments are making it much easier to register a limited liability company - what are the requirements in your country?

Instructor's Manual: An Instructor's Manual is available with additional exercises and case studies, see <www.knowledgezone.net>.

5
Buying A Business

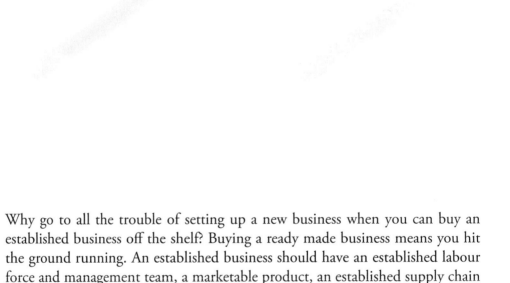

Why go to all the trouble of setting up a new business when you can buy an established business off the shelf? Buying a ready made business means you hit the ground running. An established business should have an established labour force and management team, a marketable product, an established supply chain and a loyal client base - all you need to do is jump into the driving seat and take over the controls.

The decision to own your own business is becoming more common, and this concurs with many experts who predict that a significant percentage of the workforce will be working in a self-employed capacity within the next decade.

1. Advantages of Buying a Business

There are many advantages in buying an established independent business compared with starting a new business from scratch. Consider the following points:

- there is a much lower risk of failure (these points are discussed below)
- the business should be making a profit
- the business should generate positive cashflow from the day you take over (big advantage)
- the business has products that work
- the business has demonstrable sales and marketing figures
- the business has an established customer base
- the business has an operating supply chain
- the business has trained employees and an experienced management team in place
- it should be easier to secure affordable finance.

Risk: If 50% of businesses fail within the first three years, then buying an established business must be 50% more likely to succeed as all the uncertainties of the start up phase have been removed.

Profit: The profit and loss statement will indicate if the business is making a trading profit. It takes two years on average for a start up business to become profitable, so if a business is operating profitably this probably means it has already passed the survival phase.

Cashflow: The cashflow statement will indicate the requirement for working capital. With an established business it is likely the cashflow will be positive from day one (the day you take over). Even if the cashflow is negative, you should at least know what is causing the situation and be able to see the trend and establish a budget for working capital.

Product: The manufacturing build-method and the product's features can be inspected and tested directly. Compare this with a new design which can only be model tested, or prototype tested - the designer cannot be 100% sure it will work.

Sales and Marketing: The sales and marketing figures should indicate how the product is performing in the market place. You should also look at the sales history to assess where the product's sales are on the market life-cycle profile. You do not want to buy a product that is nearing the end of its days and the sales are about to go into decline.

Customer Base: Analysing the sales figures should indicate the extent of the customer base and the amount of repeat business. Repeat business shows customer approval and indirectly reduces future marketing costs.

Supply Chain: An established business should have established good trading relationships with a number of suppliers, contractors, distributors and retailers within their supply chain. Like an established garden, these relationships take years to grow and iron out all the minor operational problems.

Personnel: An established company should have a fully trained, experienced and competent work force, together with documented work procedures, a quality control system, and an established management organisation structure.

Finance: From a financing perspective, you will have a much easier time securing capital from lenders to buy an established business, compared to funding a new business from scratch. It is estimated that less than 10% of all start up businesses are able to successfully secure the financing required at the outset. This is due to the high level of risk start up companies pose to lenders, as almost every aspect of the business is unknown and unproven.

When you buy an established business, all of the 'unknown' details should have been worked out by the previous owner. An established business should already have a solid customer base, and an experienced management team with proven processes and systems in place.

2. Disadvantages of Buying a Business

Buying a ready made business may seem like the easy option, but it does not solve all the potential problems. In fact it might actually introduce a few new problems of its own. Consider the following points:

- it takes time to find a suitable business to buy and it takes time to research the acquisition
- the high cost of buying an established business
- the risk of losing customers after buying the business.

Time Finding a Business: The time and effort it takes to look for a business to buy should be seen as a quasi cost.

Time for Due Diligence: It takes time and effort to search for hidden problems within a business. To ensure you are buying the right business you need to do a thorough investigation of its historical performance, its operations, its current status, the staff and management, the competition, the industry, and its future potential. Once the analysis has been completed, you will then have to determine how it measures up with your skills, expertise and leadership because, once you buy the business, it is then your problem (or opportunity).

The time it takes to find a suitable business and the time it takes to do due diligence should be acknowledged as quasi costs. This should be compared with the time it could take to set up your own business from scratch.

High Cost: Buying an established business is usually more expensive than starting a business from scratch. In addition to the tangible value of property, equipment and stock, there are an number of intangible costs to consider:

- what value do you give property, equipment and stock of items you cannot use and do not want, for example, old management systems, machines that need updating or obsolete stock?

- what value do you give to an established work force that may not be motivated to work for you?

- what value do you give to an established list of suppliers and an established distribution network? This should mean the supply chain is fully operational

- what value do you give to an established brand name and an established customer base? This should ensure you will have repeat business

- what cost do you assign to the expenses associated with buying a business? These expenses include; the time to find a business, the time doing due diligence, the time to audit the value of the company, and the transfer costs (consultants, lawyers, accountants and valuation specialists).

Because the business concept, organisation structure, manufacturing base, customer base and brands have already been established, the financial costs of acquiring an existing business are usually greater then starting one from scratch. As a rule of thumb, companies are valued as a multiple of annual turnover and profit.

Losing Customers: After buying a business, the new owners often find they lose 10% of their customers in the first year. This obviously devalues the goodwill component of the purchase price of the business, and raises the concern that you could lose all the loyal customers if the product is closely tied to the previous owner.

You do not want a situation where the seller leaves and most of the customers follow. For example, a hairdresser may have a loyal following of customers who will go wherever the hairdresser goes, whereas, most customers going to see a film would not have a clue who owns the cinema. You therefore need to assess how much the value of the business relates to the present owner.

There are a couple of ways to mitigate the risk of losing customers; one of them is a restraint of trade and the other is a phased transfer. A restraint of trade would prevent the seller working within x miles of the business for a number of years and, therefore, prevent the customers moving to the seller's new business. In a phased transfer, the seller agrees to continue working with the company to help the transfer of ownership. Good research, careful planning and following the advice of wise counsel are the keys to avoiding these transfer problems.

3. Reason to Sell

Try and determine why the present owner is selling - you do not want any big surprises when they hand you the key for the front door of the business. For instance, you do not want to buy a business whose competitor has just developed a new product making all YOUR stock obsolete. There may, however, be a number of genuine reasons to sell a business;

- to release capital for other business interests and commitments (for example Virgin sold their music business to finance their new airline - Virgin Atlantic)
- the owner wants to 'call it a day' and retire (leave the business completely, and use the funds for retirement)
- the owner might have lost interest in the business and want to move to some thing else
- the owner has a problem with a partner (business or domestic) and needs to sell the business to pay out the other party.

Knowing why the owner wants to sell the business may indicate the extent of their willingness to negotiate which should improve your bargaining position. (see the chapter on *Negotiation* in my book entitled *Entrepreneurs Toolkit*).

4. SWOT Analysis

SWOT stands for strengths, weaknesses, opportunities and threats. The SWOT analysis is a popular way to assess your competitive advantage and your ability to perform in the market place. The analysis enables you to develop strategies that will match your strengths and business opportunities, while limiting the impact of your weaknesses and threats. The SWOT analysis is usually presented in a matrix format.

Strengths: These are the things your business does well, where you have competitive advantage. For instance, a well known brand name has an advantage over new names entering the market.

Weaknesses: These are the things you are not so good at. For instance, the field of work may be new to you and, therefore, you have little experience in it.

Opportunities: These are the future opportunities within the field of work. For instance, you may have spotted a niche market no one else is supplying.

Threats: These are the things that could negatively impact your business. For instance, someone could open a similar business and undercut your products.

SWOT	Positive	Negative
Now	Strengths	Weaknesses
	good reputation and brand	new field / lack of experience
	latest technology and equipment	old, inefficient equipment
	fully trained staff	poor location / low traffic flow
Future	Opportunities	Threats
	an expanding market	competitors entering YOUR market
	spot unsupplied niche market	reliant on only one supplier
	outsource manufacture to reduce costs	change to keep up with new technology

Figure 5.1: SWOT Analysis Table

5. Buying a Business

After considering the pros and cons of buying a business, there are a few other issues to consider which will require more homework:

- find out as much as possible about the product. Do not rely on what the seller tells you. You need to do your own independent research and speak to potential customers, suppliers, manufacturers and even competitors
- when you are negotiating to buy a business, the price you should have in mind is **zero**! Let the seller justify why it is worth anything at all. Beware of the seller's 1/3 claim (1/3 labour costs, 1/3 fixed costs, and 1/3 profit) as this may under estimate the labour and fixed costs, but over estimate the profits.

A final word on the contract, remember to include a clause to ensure key staff stay on board, and a non-competitive clause to prevent the seller setting up a rival business in the same location.

Exercises:

1. If 50% of start up companies fail within 3 years does this mean that buying an established business is more or less likely to fail? Discuss.

2. Compare the time and effort spent finding and buying a business, compared to spotting an opportunity and starting a new business from scratch.

3. If you bought an existing business what measures would you take to keep key staff from leaving?

Instructor's Manual: An Instructor's Manual is available with additional exercises and case studies, see <www.knowledgezone.net>.

6
Buying a Franchise

Why go to all the trouble of searching for a new business idea or product when you can buy an established franchise business off the shelf? Yes, buying a franchise business has become a popular way of starting your own business. This is encouragingly supported by the statistics that show franchise businesses are more likely to be successful than independent start up businesses - so this option is definitely worth considering.

Buying a franchise business means you are buying the rights to start a business with a brand name and product which are already developed and established in the market place. The big advantage of buying a franchise is that it is usually a much faster way of expanding your business compared with starting from scratch and growing a business on your own, with your own funds. And, because you are effectively running your own business, you are still benefiting from your own drive, motivation, determination and ingenuity.

Buying into a franchise business enables you to hit the ground running (no time is lost setting up the business concept). A franchise business could be an established company like the classic McDonald's or Starbucks which franchise the rights to you to sell their burgers or their coffee under their brand name, their product menu and their management system. The franchisor (in this case McDonald's or Starbucks) will give the franchisee (that is you) an established business framework to operate from. They will train your staff and give them detailed procedures to follow; they will supply you with all the stationary and logos etc. Essentially they provide everything you should need to run the business. In return, you pay the franchisor a signing fee and a percentage of your turnover.

1. Advantages of Buying a Franchise Business

Buying into a franchise business is a big decision, certainly a big financial investment and a commitment of your time. So it is important to be aware of the pros and cons to enable you to make an informed decision. Some of the advantages of buying a franchise are:

- the franchise business you buy into will have a tried and tested product with proof that it sells - you can see the other franchisees' sales figures
- franchise businesses have a higher success rate compared to independent start up businesses. This means the business risk is lower and, further, the proven track record should make it easier to secure bank loans
- the market research undertaken by the franchisor, and the sales figures from the existing franchisees, will show how the product is performing in other locations. This should give you some indication of how the product might perform in your location
- you are buying into a proven company and product with a known brand name and established reputation
- the franchisor can pool the franchisees' fees together to share the marketing, advertising and promotion costs. National marketing will help to establish a strong brand name nationwide which, in turn, helps to develop interest in your local area
- the franchisees, as a group, can buy in bulk which will give them greater buying power and lower prices from the suppliers
- the franchisor will help you find a good location for your business based on demographics, traffic flows, business counts, growth areas and their experience with the other franchisees. If you are a fashion retailer, for example, the franchisor knows you need to be located on the High Street where there is good traffic flow

- the franchisor can act as a business mentor, providing advice during the early stages on how to get your business up and running. The franchisor's head office usually provides a team of experts you can approach when you have a problem or need a sounding board. Head office staff may even end up becoming your agony aunt, business adviser and extended member of your family!

- training is provided by the franchisor to get you and your staff up and running. This could be one or two weeks at the head office training centre, plus in-store training at a mentor franchisee's facility, plus in-store training in your own facility to confirm you are making the product correctly. This training is generally technical, operational, managerial, and sales and marketing

- a franchise pack is usually provided which includes stationary and other business requirements (letter heads, business cards, invoice books, receipt books, menus, price lists), together with signage, uniforms and promotional material.

Franchise businesses have a certain look and feel about them. Customers seem to prefer to buy from companies they feel are established and successful and, if they see these outlets in more than one place, this helps to reinforce the brand.

2. Disadvantages of Buying a Franchise

Although statistically franchise businesses have a higher success rate than the independent sole trader start ups, there are a number of concerns which should be considered, particularly by the true entrepreneur:

- buying into an established franchise business with a track record will probably be more expensive than setting up an independent business on your own. Therefore, initially, the financial risk will be higher because you have more at stake

- trading is usually limited by geographical area as specified in the franchise agreement, this may limit your business' growth potential

- the franchisor may not be too concerned about the competition from other businesses in your location selling the same product, or even other branches of the same franchise - have you noticed there is often more than one McDonald's in the same town? After all it is your funds at risk!

- your scope for opportunity and innovation might be limited because the franchise operates to a strict formula for material supply, production, sales and marketing - the franchisor might not want the franchisees to be too enterprising. This might not suit the **true entrepreneur** who might want to pursue business opportunities as they are spotted, and strike while the iron is hot

- there is always the potential for conflict between the franchisee (you) and the franchisor (them)
- although you may be funding your operation you are not really your own boss because you are having to follow the franchisor's rules. And, being independent may have been one of the prime reasons for starting your own business in the first place.

A final point to be aware of is that there may be limitations in the franchise agreement on selling your franchise business to someone else.

3. Establishing Your Own Franchise Business

In the process of setting up a new business, you might hit on a great idea for an innovative product that you feel is suitable to be franchised. This will enable you to become a franchisor and gain leverage through the efforts of the franchisees. But, before you can start selling franchise licences, you need to establish your product and your company so that you have something tangible to show potential franchisees. You will also have to develop franchise business management systems for the franchisees to follow, together with training manuals, technical support, advertising and promotions.

There are many **advantages** to selling YOUR franchise ideas and products to franchisees. Consider the following points and ways to gain leverage:

• the franchisees pay you for the rights to sell your product (thank you very much!)

• your business grows through the effort of other people (the franchisees), using their money and their time. This is a great way to gain leverage with little risk to yourself

".... I'm thinking of setting up a franchise business - any ideas ....?"

- the franchisees pay you through their fees to market YOUR product, which further helps to establish YOUR brand!
- the franchisees collectively give YOU the buying power of a big business
- the franchisees take the risk for setting up their business. If a franchise fails they lose their money not yours.

By setting up a franchise business you are effectively selling your creative ideas and business concepts.

4. Disadvantages of Establishing a Franchise

Although setting up a franchise is a great way to gain leverage through the efforts and investments of the franchisees, it should be acknowledged that setting up a franchise requires a considerable amount of effort. Consider the following points:

- setting up a franchise business is a big investment in time and money. It could take over a year to develop all the business management, manufacturing and legal components - these are all up front costs
- it could take many years to get a return on your investment
- it takes a special skill to structure and document the nature of your business and present it in an easy to understand form for the franchisees to follow
- you will need to develop an operating manual outlining the what, why and when
- you will need to write training programmes for the different positions in the franchise organisation structure
- you will need to employ the services of an accountant to check your business plan and confirm the new franchise venture is financially feasible
- you will need to employ a solicitor who specialises in franchise agreements to write the franchise contract. The contract needs to be watertight, setting out the obligations of each party, including how the fees, mark-ups on supplied goods and any other payments from the franchisee are to be calculated
- conflicts could arise if the obligations between the parties are not clearly defined at the outset
- developing your business into a franchise will reduce the amount of time you have available to run your own business. If you have to employ a manager to run your business this should be seen as a quasi cost

- being a franchisor requires different types of business and management skills. You could be a very successful owner of a business making pizzas, but if you start franchising you effectively move out of pizza making and into being a franchisor managing a chain of franchise businesses.

The franchise business is only as good as the strength of all the outlets put together. If you have one rogue store this could be the weak link that quickly destroys the brand. This famously happened with **Arthur Andersen,** an accounting firm. One of the American branches of Arthur Andersen was **Enron's** accountant! After Enron's fraud became public Arthur Andersen's branches around the world quickly imploded and closed.

The Arthur Andersen accountants were found guilty of obstructing a government investigation into the collapse of Enron. It was reported that employees destroyed documents concerning the energy group by the truckload. Consequently, Arthur Andersen had little information to hand over when issued with a subpoena by the US Securities and Exchange commission in 2001. The verdict in 2002 led to Arthur Andersen's disintegration, leading to the loss of 28,000 jobs around the world. The company has since (in 2005) been cleared by the Supreme Court, but the damage was done.

Exercises:

1. Conduct a visual survey in your area and list all the companies that have the look and feel of a franchise business.

2. Consider a franchise business in your area and discuss why it has or has not been successful.

3. Outline a business plan to franchise a product you are familiar with and sell the franchise rights.

Instructor's Manual: An Instructor's Manual is available with additional exercises and case studies, see <www.knowledgezone.net>.

7
Family Business

Many small businesses want to *'keep it in the family'* – be it the corner shop, Steptoe and Son's scrapyard, or even the great Sky TV corporation. Nepotism is a natural instinct that encourages people to do the best for their family and relations.

But keeping it in the family can be a double edged sword - on the one hand it is a secure job on a plate with good career prospects, but on the other hand, the family business may limit the budding entrepreneur's scope for exploring new opportunities, investment and growth.

The importance of small businesses in general, and family businesses in particular, usually falls below the MBA radar of interest, as the MBA programmes tend to focus on the management issues of large corporations. But this is changing, as the small businesses and family businesses start to speak with one voice. When you group all the small businesses and family businesses together you see a sleeping giant underpinning the local economy.

1. Family Business Characteristics

The definition of a family business seems fairly obvious in its wider context - family members working together. However, what is more important are the characteristics of a typical family business.

Family businesses tend to be small concerns with respect to the revenue they generate and the number of people they employ. They also tend to employ the youngest and oldest members of the family. The older established small businesses tend to be more likely to survive in the long term, but less likely to grow. They are therefore unlikely to generate new sources of employment, particularly for the youngest family members as they leave school. Like the young elephant bulls in Africa, once the younger members of the family have learnt how to fend for themselves they are usually thrown out of the herd to find new pastures.

Lifestyle Businesses: A high percentage of family businesses fall into the lifestyle category. Lifestyle businesses are set up, primarily, to undertake an activity that the owner-manager (and family) enjoys whilst also providing an adequate income for the family.

Family businesses are not usually set up for rapid growth, therefore, once they reach a level of activity that provides an adequate income, the management typically becomes routine and tactical. If they do want the business to grow, the funds are generally sourced from retained profits rather than from outside venture capital. This should enable a comfortable and manageable level of sustainable growth, without the pressure of having to repay investment loans.

".... I've got one son running my company in Sydney, another in London and my daughter running my company in Beijing...."

2. Family Support

Family support, in its wider sense, is an important source of encouragement, motivation, recognition and finance for start up businesses. Family and relations are two of the start up entrepreneur's main sources of finance. In this situation, although the entrepreneur may not join the family business directly, the entrepreneur will definitely benefit from the family network in other ways.

3. Family Link

Researchers have found a link between the budding entrepreneur and the entrepreneur's family. If the father was a small business entrepreneur then his children are more likely to follow in his foot steps and also become small business entrepreneurs.

Children brought up in the close proximity of their entrepreneurial parents will obviously be influenced by the small business working environment. The 'table talk' would establish small business norms and expectations. The children would see their parents making and promoting their products and would probably be asked to help in the business from time to time - all hands to the pumps.

But, will the siblings join the family business? Possibly not if they think their parents are out of touch with new technology. Have you noticed that you never see 'and Son' on company names these days. It's no longer cool.

".... one day Rodney all this will all be yours..."

4. Problems Employing Family Members

Although there is generally an expectation that you can trust family members (because they come from a good home!), in reality there are a number of problems associated with employing family members:

Family Favours: Being asked to employ a family member's son or daughter during the summer holidays is one thing, but offering them long term employment can be a different matter. A temporary job could easily be perceived as getting a foot on the bottom rung of their career ladder within your company.

Employment Rules: Employment rules and regulations should apply equally to all your employees. If some family members think that just because they are related they can take advantage of the rules, you need to sort that out immediately. If you allow family members to break the rules this could create a climate of mistrust among the non-family members.

Performance Review: Family members, like other employees working in the company, should have regular performance reviews and should know what level of skill is required of them before they are eligible for pay rises and promotions. They need to agree on a training schedule and target dates for proficiency. If this does not happen, family members could develop unrealistic expectations with respect to fast track promotion and top end salaries.

Complaints Procedure: If employees have a problem, they would normally bring it to the attention of their immediate supervisor rather than the head of the company. This procedure can become blurred when it is a family member who has the problem. In the interest of fair play, family complaints should be dealt with in the same way as complaints from non-family employees.

As family businesses shake off the old image of corner shop keepers, so they are starting to find their voice as major employers in the economy.

Exercises:

1. Discuss why family businesses, collectively, are said to be major employers in the economy.

2. Conduct an informal survey of family businesses in your area to find out why people prefer to work within their own small family business.

3. Discuss how family members can support other family members to start up their own business.

Instructors Manual: An Instructor's Manual is available with additional exercises and case studies, see <www.knowledgezone.net>.

 cosmic mba series

8
Working From Home

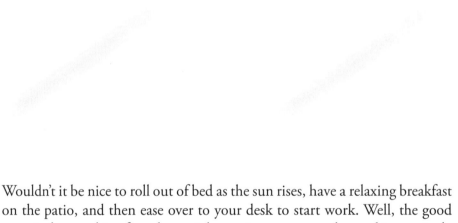

Wouldn't it be nice to roll out of bed as the sun rises, have a relaxing breakfast on the patio, and then ease over to your desk to start work. Well, the good news is that working from home is becoming more popular, and increasingly becoming more feasible with new technology, new types of products and new ways of doing business.

Garages, spare bedrooms, and even the garden shed are being converted into work places and offices. There are many examples of successful businesses which started from such humble beginnings. HP (Hewlett Packard) computers, for example, was a garage start up, and the corporation has since bought the old garage at 376 Addison Ave, Palo Alto, to remind them of their humble origins.

Richard Branson is another highly successful entrepreneur who started from modest beginnings. Branson is reported to have started his second-hand record mail-order business from a public telephone box - this certainly cut down his overheads! With business success, Branson first moved to a river boat on the Thames, and then, before the river boat sank, his staff forced him to move into a more substantial Head Office in London.

1. Changing Work Environment

There are a number of factors which are changing the way we work. These changes are partly due to improved facilities (particularly mobile communications and the Internet), and partly due to the deregulation and privatisation of nationalised industries and monopolies. This has led to the breakdown of large industrial corporations into many smaller companies. These changes have freed up the market, enabling entrepreneurs to compete on a level playing field. For example:

- communication facilities have evolved from telegraph, voice and fax, to emails and the Internet (broadband)
- mobile phones, wi-fi and Blackberrys are breaking the link with landlines, making the mobile office a feasible option
- deregulation and privatisation are forcing the national telecom companies to compete without protection. This has led to improved communication facilities, improved services, and reduced tariffs. Internet and international telephone calls are now considered relatively minor business costs
- with the bulk of manufacturing moving to the East (Asia), this has freed up the markets in the West (America and Europe), allowing the small business entrepreneur to focus on new and diverse business opportunities
- increasing affluence is encouraging many of us to put a meaningful lifestyle before earning mega-bucks.

"....I'll just pop a copy of 'Sergeant Pepper' in the post for you...."

2. Benefits of Working From Home

Giving up the day job to work from home is a big decision so it is important to be aware of the pros and cons before taking the leap. Consider some of the advantages:

- working from home is an obvious starting point for a small business as it reduces the overheads - there is no office rent (assuming you are using a room in your home) and there are no additional telephone line rentals
- working from home, maybe part-time, gives the entrepreneur time to test the market and grow the business incrementally before taking the leap into expensive business premises
- there is no 'dead-time' travelling to the office. This could be a big time saver. For some people this may be more than a couple of hours a day of productive time gained
- there are no travelling costs – car, buses, trains or ferries
- working from home should be a much healthier environment because you have less contact with other people. Therefore, this should lower your chances of picking up a winter cold and other contagious bugs
- working from home should enable you to be more flexible with your time to suit your lifestyle
- flexible working hours are particularly useful when bringing up children or caring for elderly parents. For example, a couple working from home could can take it in turns to look after the family members
- clients visiting the 'home' office has become more acceptable - working from home is no longer seen as an amateurish arrangement
- if it is not appropriate to have a business meeting at home you can always use one of the many coffee shops that have become trendy business meeting venues
- the introduction of broadband has given the home business high speed Internet
- web conferencing enables virtual meetings where you can remain an active member of the business team
- flexible working conditions increases job satisfaction
- working from home, surrounded by your home comforts, can be a much quieter and more inspirational environment compared to a hectic open plan office. At home you are much closer to your personal library of reference material
- companies might actually prefer you to work from home, because it is expensive to provide staff with a permanent office. The trend is to have hot desk work stations linked to the network which can be accessed from anywhere within the company's building and even from home via the Internet
- as more people work from home, so all the basic business support services are becoming locally available.

3. Disadvantages of Working From Home

Although there are many advantages working from home, there are also a number of concerns which should be considered:

- family and friends might not fully understand the implications of a home office where you require uninterrupted work time, even though you are at home
- a noisy family could be a distraction when you need to concentrate
- if you are using the spare room this could be seen as a quasi cost (because you cannot rent the room to someone else)
- the travelling time to your office can be productive - with a notebook computer you can catch-up with your work, and with wi-fi you can catch-up with your emails
- walking to work may be your only regular exercise. Without this enforced exercise, working from home could become very sedentary and unhealthy
- flexible time may become too flexible and therefore less productive, particularly if you need the discipline of a 9-5 job. For example, without the pressure to get back to your office, lunch breaks could become two or three hours
- some employers view working from home as 'skiving off', even though you are still producing the goods - it is an old fashioned perception that is difficult to change
- working from home could be '*out of sight out of mind*' when it comes to salary review and promotion time.

If working at home means working on your own, this raises a number of concerns about your competency and lack of team support. Consider the following:

- if you are working at home on your own, do you have the ability to do the job? And, if you need help, is telephone technical support enough?
- how will you motivate yourself to perform? Some people need other team members to motivate them to go the extra mile
- if your type of work needs creative input, you might miss the cross-flow of creative ideas; miss the interaction to help solve problems; miss the sounding board to bounce ideas off; and miss the team synergy. In fact working on your own at home could mean you are working in a creative vacuum.

Working TOO Hard!: Not only do you need the discipline to work when other tasks (such as gardening or shopping) are competing for your attention, but you also need the discipline to stop working to ensure a balanced life. To be more productive sometimes means you actually have to stop work to recharge. If you

continue to plod on, you not only tire yourself out and get less done, but also start making silly mistakes. Sometimes you have to walk away and take care of yourself, mentally and physically, and then come back refreshed and revitalised to work more productively.

Home based entrepreneurs are known for working too much, risking burnout. As the *Peter's Principle* states '...*work usually expands to fill the time available...*' consequently you end up working every hour of the day chasing your tail. Setting and keeping business hours is a great tool for some to increase their focus and productivity.

Labour Rate: Your labour rate could be lower working from home compared to employees working in large corporations. This is because the labour rate is often linked to investment, and large corporations have more funds to invest in R&D, production equipment, machinery and plant to maintain their competitive advantage.

Working from home in a lifestyle business might make it difficult to value your labour rate. If you value your labour rate too low this might lead to you doing menial jobs to save on direct costs, whereas you could be making more money if you worked directly on your product and outsourced the rest.

Networking: Many companies thrive on informal communication and informal networking. Working from home means you will miss out on the office banter around the coffee machine and after work drinks.

IT Support: Large companies have IT departments to sort out computer problems (such as viruses and security threats). When working from home you will either have to employ a local expert, or waste your own valuable time trying to fix problems that could take you twice as long as the experts.

Large companies have IT departments which constantly back-up the data on the computer network. When you work at home you will have to set up your own system. This will incur equipment costs, your time (quasi cost), and require discipline to back up the information regularly.

Having considered all the pros and cons, there may be a happy medium where you can split your work between your corporate office, your home lifestyle office, and your mobile office - giving you the best of all worlds.

4. Mobile Office

Mobile phones, portable notebook computers and wi-fi communication networks are making the mobile office a feasible reality. These mobile facilities are not only enabling managers to stay in touch with their head office while on business trips, but actually enable managers to take their office with them.

Mobile facilities enable communication with the head office, clients, suppliers and contractors while on the move. The mobile office could be an Internet cafe, an airport lounge (or any wi-fi hotspot), the entrepreneur's car, their campervan or even their yacht. Consider the following points:

- the mobile office frees the self-employed salesperson from their corporate desk so they can actually spend more time on the road visiting clients
- mobile conferencing enables managers to attend virtual meetings with their business team and clients. Regular virtual meetings should keep a scattered team linked and working together
- working from your mobile home as you drive around the countryside enables you to strike a balance between your work and your lifestyle.

Even corporate managers can benefit from mobile office facilities while they are on an extended business trip or a holiday. They are able to relax knowing everything is okay back at the head office, and if there is a problem they have the opportunity to nip it in the bud. They can also keep on top of their emails while they are away to avoid being greeted by a few hundred emails on their first day back at work. Holidays in the bush and flying time no longer need to be vacuum periods without any business contact.

Mobile technology has given us the flexibility to write our books on the move. This book was actually written on the chart table on our yacht in the South Pacific which we use as a mobile office as we cruise the islands.

Exercises:

1. Rank the reasons why you would prefer to work from home in preference to working in a grand office in the city.

2. Discuss the disadvantages of working from home.

3. Discuss what equipment you would need to operate a mobile office for your line of work.

Instructor's Manual: An Instructor's Manual is available with additional exercises and case studies, see <www.knowledgezone.net>.

9
Selling Techniques

The sales functions and the marketing functions are two sides of the same coin, as one relates to the other. Marketing is the management function to make people aware of the company and its products and create an interest, while the sales function is to close the deal and make the sale. The two functions obviously have to go hand-in-hand. The marketing function is discussed in detail in my book *Entrepreneurs Toolkit*, where it focuses on:

- market research techniques to determine what the customer wants
- how to identify and quantify the competition
- speed to market (to beat your competitor)
- determining a pricing strategy
- locating a business to achieve good passing trade
- promotion and advertising.

This chapter will focus on the selling techniques the small business entrepreneur can use to turn a lead into a sale. Although the days of the **foot in the door salesman** with a suitcase full of dodgy products are gone, customers still do respond to the charismatic salesperson.

Many managers shy away from selling their product because they fear rejection. Some people take rejection in their stride, while others get deeply upset. In reality the **customer link** in the supply chain is probably the most important and most powerful link. If you control the customer link, then you are at the top of the food chain, and all the other companies in the supply chain have to sell their products through you.

".... Hello .... I have a new product which will make you a fortune ...."

1. Become a Customer

Becoming a customer for the products and services you are selling will help you gain a different perspective of your business - the customer's perspective. This role reversal puts yourself in 'their' shoes which might help you to see directly if you could improve on the way your business is selling its products. For example, if you have a boutique selling the latest fashion, go to a competitor's boutique and note how you are approached and helped by the sales staff.

To be successful entrepreneurs need to know what their customers want. Are the customers buying on features and price, or are they buying on quality and service? These are often at opposite ends of the product continuum.

In today's consumer society, the customers' expectations are continually being increased to expect the products to have the latest features and packaging, as well as bigger discounts, lower prices and better terms and conditions. It is essential to know how the customer is reacting so you can align your products and services to the customers' needs.

2. Cold Calling

There are not many things in life that make the toughest person break out into a cold sweat, but public speaking and cold calling are two such situations. Cold calling is the unsolicited call from the seller (you) to a potential customer. When the person you are calling answers the phone they are not expecting your call and they do not know who you are. This means you only have a few seconds to introduce yourself and start selling your product.

Since writing this chapter I have become more sympathetic to cold calling tele-marketers who must be facing rejection all the time. They are usually very polished, straight to the point and have you answering questions before you realise what is happening.

Before cold calling you need to develop your selling strategy, otherwise you will not only waste your valuable time, but also the valuable time of your prospective customers. A typical selling approach would be;

- identify the sectors of the market that could buy your product
- list companies that could buy your product
- list people within the companies that could buy your product
- prepare your sales pitch.

"Hello .... I would like to introduce myself ...."

Small business entrepreneurs tend to do well when they focus on a small niche market, leaving the broad global saturation marketing to the big boys. With a list of possible client companies in hand, the next challenge is to find the names of the people who could buy your product. It is frustrating to deal with someone who has to continually refer to someone else to make a decision. It is often best to start at the top and work down - you can at least say that the boss told you to speak to them.

Before picking up the phone you must know exactly what you are going to say because you only have a few seconds to gain the person's interest. Get straight to the point with your name, company name, product description and how it will benefit them and benefit their clients.

The first challenge is to get past the receptionist. If your approach is flustered and uncertain, you will be politely declined. So get straight to the point *"Hello, this is Joe Bloggs from Bloggs equipment, I would like to speak to <name> about our new product."*

Or better, if you have been able to email them first you can say .... *"Hello, this is Joe Bloggs from Bloggs equipment, I would like to speak to <name>, I am following up on my email"*. Even better still, if you can, say you are replying to their email.

When you get through to the manager never start with *"I am sorry to bother you"*. It may be polite but it is weak and not a good image to start the sales pitch. It is better to be enthusiastic about all the benefits your customer can gain from your product, and be excited at the prospect of meeting them. Try and word your questions so the person answers **"yes"**, never "no". For example;

"Hello, this is Joe Bloggs from Bloggs equipment. My company has just designed a new machine which will be able to reduce your production costs by 30% [this is the hook], *I am going to be in your area next week and would be pleased to give you a 20 minute demonstration. Would ten o'clock on Tuesday be okay for you?"*

Besides trying to organise a meeting you might send the customer a brochure or sample of the product. The bottom line is that you have to give the prospective customer sufficient information for them to make an informed decision.

Most people hate cold calling, but cold calling could be the key to developing a comprehensive data base of contacts who could become clients. You can be assured most successful entrepreneurs have had to use cold calling to develop their extensive network of contacts.

3. Selling Techniques

Having expended much time and effort trying to find potential customers (by whatever means), now is the opportunity for the entrepreneur to introduce them to great products and slick services, close the deal and make the sale.

Part of the selling technique is to clarify the difference between your product's great '*features*' and the realistic '*benefits*' to the customer. Features refer to a product's whistles and bells, while the benefits refer to the characteristics of the product which will help solve the customer's problems. Ultimately customers buy solutions. Therefore, before you can accurately show how the product will benefit the client, you have to gain an understanding of the client's needs or problems.

It is the entrepreneur's challenge to translate the product's features into how the product will increase the customer's competitive advantage and/or enhance their lifestyle, by showing that the product may be quicker, cheaper, more efficient, easier to operate, make less mistakes, or is fully automatic.

Making a **presentation** is an excellent opportunity for the entrepreneur sales person to communicate the potential benefits of their product to the customer. It is essential that the entrepreneur gets the point across so the customer clearly understands the potential of the product to meet their needs and solve their problems.

With the increasing complexity of consumer products, particularly electronic products which are updated every six months, customers are becoming overwhelmed with technical data. This is a great opportunity for the entrepreneur to gain the customer's confidence and guide them through the product selection process - it is essential to make it easy for the customer to make a decision.

Research has shown that, if a person has too many products to choose from, they have difficulty making a decision and will either flick a coin, or walk away. Have you noticed how supermarkets often bombard us with far too many choices - how can there be so many different types of tea?! Therefore it is important to reduce the customer's choice to decide between A or B.

With so much competition, it is vital to look for ways to distinguish yourself and your product from the competition. One way is to explain how your product can add value to the customer's business. This is usually quantified by how your product will reduce the customer's costs or increase revenue, but also outline how your company can help with the installation of the product and training of staff. You can also help the customer calculate the breakeven point to recover their set up costs, together with providing financial arrangements - it is a mistake to assume the customer only focuses on price.

4. Business Cards

When you meet a prospective customer, exchanging business cards is often the first opportunity you have to create an image of yourself and your company - it is almost a ritual. Not only does it help you remember each others names, positions, business names and contact details, but together with the logo and artwork, the business card conveys a brand image.

Check out the other business cards in your profession as they can vary considerably. For example, estate agents often include a photograph of themselves, but you would not expect to see this on the business card of a lawyer or doctor. And you would be surprised if a surgeon displayed the tools of his trade!

In publishing, for example, an author's business card often includes a picture of the book cover. This should be relatively straight forward to produce as the artwork for the cover is already done, and the detail should help to portray a professional image.

Product Brochure: Explaining your product or service to a potential customer is so much easier if you have a brochure, flyer or prospectus with attractive artwork and clear explanatory photographs and diagrams. It allows the customer to collect information from a number of suppliers and make their decision later. The brochure should guide the potential customer to the company's web site.

Web Site: It is now expected that companies and their products should have a presence on the Internet. The web site could simply be a replica of the company's brochure, but web sites can offer much more. They can be interactive, updated as required, and linked to a regular mail shot.

Exercises:

1. Put yourself in your customer's shoes and become a customer for your type of product. Critically appraise the sales staff's performance.

2. Discuss your cold calling approach.

3. Discuss your selling technique.

Instructor's Manual: An Instructor's Manual is available with additional exercises and case studies, see <www.knowledgezone.net>.

10
Customer Service

When I was a student, I remember opening a Mars bar and being disappointed to see the chocolate was slightly discoloured. I had a couple of bites, wrapped it up and posted it to Mars. Within a week I received a parcel containing three new Mars bars - I was really chuffed.

That type of customer service response was rare in those days, but today, in a more competitive and educated market, companies cannot afford to lose potential customers and repeat business. In fact, if the customer takes the time and effort to complain to the company, there is a good chance they can be converted to actually become a supporter of the company and its products.

".... a Mars a day helps you work rest and play ...."

The customer service department is the customer's front door to your company. This is the department the customer will initially contact if they have a problem, need information or wish to make a comment. It is therefore essential to have an 0800 number on the product for the customers to ring.

All too often, within a company, the customer service department is perceived as a separate office working in a world of its own. However, as figure 10.1 shows, the customer service department is central to the company's operation. They are the main source of customer feedback, and an early warning flag for technical and legal problems.

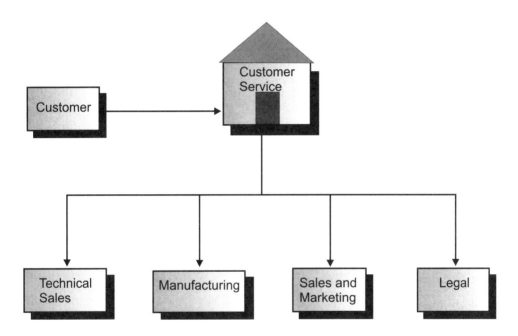

Figure 10.1: Customer Service Communication Flow Chart

When a customer contacts a company they judge the company by the person they speak to. It is therefore important that the customer service representative has excellent communication skills and access to relevant information. It is also important to ensure that all staff who deal directly with the customers are trained in customer service - you do not want them arguing with your valued customers.

In most companies customer service is the first department to receive requests for information, directions on how to use the products, and complaints if a product is not working properly. The customer service department needs to establish what category the enquiry falls into:

- technical sales
- technical product support
- a design problem
- a manufacturing problem
- a warranty and liability implication.

If the customer's enquiry is for technical information about a product, customer service needs to direct them to the technical sales team. If the customer's enquiry is concerning a problem with the product, 'someone' needs to determine if this is due to;

- a design fault
- a faulty batch of materials
- a manufacturing fault
- a packaging fault
- a distribution fault
- a retailing fault.

It is critically important to communicate this information to the relevant department for prompt action. The company needs to quickly establish if the problem is a one off, or relates to the whole batch. If it is a problem affecting the whole production run, this could result in a costly product recall.

1. Technical Sales

What product should I buy? How big? How fast? What features? How will it interface with my existing equipment? As products become more mind blowingly complicated and high tech, with upgrades every six months, customers need someone they can trust to guide them through the selection process.

2. Technical Support

"*I cannot get my new gadget to work.*" How often does this happen? As the operation of consumer products is becoming more technical and less intuitive, so the customer will increasingly need more technical support to help them get started. There is nothing more frustrating than buying the latest top of the range product only to take it home and find that you cannot get it to work.

Documentation: In the haste to deliver the product to market, it would seem some manufacturers leave the supporting documentation (operating instructions and repair manuals) to the last minute. Documentation and after sales service is becoming an important sales issue because consumers know from bitter experience the difficulties they have had with products in the past.

Telephone Support: International companies such as Dell Computers have set the standard for telephone support from anywhere in the world. As this becomes a customer requirement, all companies will eventually offer similar support. It is not always convenient or possible for the customer to return the product to the retailer, and impossible if the product was purchased through the Internet!

3. Design Problem

In the rush to get the product to market the design process might have been fast tracked, cutting back on model testing and prototype (beta) testing. Consequently inherent design faults might not have been picked up. If there **are** any design faults this information needs to be immediately communicated to the design office so the design can be updated. The design office needs to simulate the problem to ensure there are no safety implications. If there are, this information needs to be communicated to the CEO for prompt action.

".... we are just testing our new car for the world market ...."

4. Manufacturing Problem

The manufacturing process is usually a dynamic balance of mechanical settings which are constantly changing. Consequently machinery needs to be monitored by sharp eyed operators who are regularly checking that the settings and outputs are within tolerance. If this does not happen and quality control do not pick-up the errors, then these mistakes will be sent straight to the customer.

With the increasing amount of manufacturing being outsourced offshore, quality management is becoming a major concern for companies, particularly as they might not see any of their products except to approve a test batch. It is becoming common practice to ship the product straight from the manufacturer (offshore) to the distributor or customer.

5. Product Liability

We have Ralph Nader in America to thank for forcing some stubborn car manufacturers to face up to their product liability. He successfully challenged a major car manufacturer about an inherent design fault. Nader found that, in the event of an accident, the position of the car's fuel tank could lead to a fire and the death of trapped passengers.

In an article entitled '*The Safe Car You Can't Buy*' published in 1959, he concluded, "*It is clear Detroit today is designing automobiles for style, cost, performance, and calculated obsolescence, but not - despite the 5,000,000 reported accidents, nearly 40,000 fatalities, 110,000 permanent disabilities, and 1,500,000 injuries yearly - for safety.*"

In 1965, he published *Unsafe at Any Speed*, a best-selling indictment of the auto industry and its poor safety standards. He specifically targeted General Motors' Corvair.

Car manufacturers now react very quickly to design and production line faults and will recall all the vehicles affected if they are concerned the fault could have safety implications.

6. Marketing

Having gone to the expense and effort of promoting and selling your products you should have a good feel for the cost of making a sale.

Cost of a sale = $\dfrac{\text{Sales and Marketing Costs}}{\text{Number of Products Sold}}$

For every sale there is the prospect of repeat business and referrals to new customers. It therefore makes financial sense, if nothing else, to keep your customers happy and if there are any complaints, these should be resolved immediately.

Handling complaints effectively can turn a dissatisfied customer into a loyal customer. Consider the following:

- attracting new customers is costly and unpredictable - repeat business from existing customers is far easier to attract
- customers who have received good service may well recommend your company to others, but customers who feel badly treated are likely to complain about your company instead
- as a small business entrepreneur, you will probably not have national advertising campaigns to boost your image. Therefore, you need to make sure that word-of-mouth publicity is positive, particularly if you rely heavily on local business.

Having a smooth running customer service department responding personally to the clients' needs is a great opportunity to gain competitive advantage.

Exercises:

1. Consider your personal experience with customer service departments. Do you have any recommendations?

2. If a customer complains about your product, how would you try and turn them into a loyal customer?

3. If a customer finds a manufacturing fault with your product how would you respond?

Instructor's Manual: Instructor's Manual: An Instructor's Manual is available with additional exercises and case studies, see <www.knowledgezone.net>.

11
Outsourcing

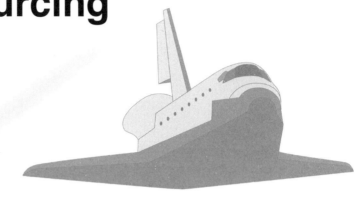

Outsourcing is the process of contracting out work to another company that specialises in that particular field of work. Offshoring is the process of contracting out work to an overseas company (typically IT work to India and manufacturing to China).

The volume of work being outsourced offshore is increasing due to the beneficial cost differentials between labour costs. These costs are significantly less in the East (Asia) compared to the West (America and Europe). Companies operating in a competitive market are almost forced to outsource their work offshore if they want to be competitive on price. For example, Dyson outsources the manufacturing of his cleaners to Malaysia, while keeping his design and marketing team at the head office in the UK.

With this arrangement Dyson is able to compete on price and product features enabling his company to expand into new markets (especially America) where his products would have otherwise been too expensive. By subdividing his company this way Dyson has shrewdly kept control of both the front end (R&D and design) and the last link in the supply chain (sales and marketing), while outsourcing offshore all the manufacturing to reduce costs and gain competitive advantage.

Small business entrepreneurs should see outsourcing as a great opportunity, enabling them to acquire work in their field of expertise from large companies that want to reduce their costs. The health service, for example, outsources cleaning, maintenance, security and, in some countries, the management of the health service itself.

Small business entrepreneurs can also outsource their work to outside companies that can do the work more quickly and cheaply. This will enable entrepreneurs to expand their product range without having to invest in capital equipment and train additional staff.

The bottom line is that outsourcing reduces set up costs and makes small businesses even more flexible and competitive.

1. The Change From In-House to Outsource

Privatisation and deregulation are revolutionising the way we work, the extent of these changes has not been seen since the early days of the industrial revolution. Large nationalised industries and large monopolistic corporations used to expand

in every direction - like an octopus their tentacles would reach out to take over everything they touched. This is all changing - deregulation is freeing up the market for entrepreneurs to introduce new technology, new products and more efficient working practices, which includes outsourcing and offshoring.

"....my house has never been so clean since I invented the Dyson!!"

In the past, large companies would never have thought of letting an outside company do their accounts, payroll and security, but now, as managers cut out corporate bureaucracy and inefficiencies, outsourcing of non-core activities has become commonplace. The key to outsourcing is to achieve competitive advantage through leverage of:

• range of expertise
• reduced capital expenditure of equipment
• reduced staff training and supervision.

For example, when we fly with BA '*the world's favourite airline*' or Virgin Atlantic '*the world's trendiest airline*', we feel we are buying a service from that particular company, but in reality, some or all of their services will have been outsourced. Even though the check-in staff, cabin crew and pilots wear stylish corporate branded uniforms, they may well be agency staff subcontracted to that particular airline. And, further, the onboard maintenance, catering and cleaning services will also have been outsourced to local companies.

2. What Jobs Can Be Offshored

Over the past forty years the industries that pioneered the industrial revolution (shipbuilding, iron and steel, textiles and clothing, and car manufacturing) have all been offshored to countries such as Japan, Korea and China.

Today's improved telecommunication facilities have been the catalyst to outsourcing thousands of administration jobs offshore. In the 1980s, the concept of outsourcing started with the 'back office' jobs (accounts and purchase orders), but now the trend is to offshore 'front office' call centres and tele-marketing jobs as well. Is any job safe?

Workers who previously thought they had secure administration and service type jobs are sensing that their positions could be next to go. And, when the journalists and media see their work being offshored, then the disaster will be official.

"…. Hello British Rail, the next train leaving Birmingham is …."

Bangalore
Call Centre

The general criteria for outsourcing offshore is that the work:
- does not require direct customer interaction (face-to-face)
- can be teleworked
- has a high information content
- is easy to set up
- is repetitive (easier to train)
- can be offered at a lower cost (this is due to the wage differentials between the two countries).

The driving factor behind outsourcing offshore has been the need to cut production costs to stay competitive - particularly during economic recessions. The enabling factor has been the global electronic telecom network that allows voice and digital data to be transmitted instantly anywhere in the world at negligible cost.

3. Benefits of Outsourcing and Offshoring

Outsourcing, offshoring and sticking to core-business activities seem to go in cycles with the economy. Outsourcing is currently the flavour of the month for the following reasons;
- it lowers manufacturing costs
- it lowers internal capital expenditure on equipment
- it lowers internal training and supervision costs
- a smaller work force means less supervision, less admin, and smaller premises which all combine to lower the overhead costs
- with the above cost savings there should be additional funds available to finance R&D and capital equipment
- it releases funds to pursue new business opportunities.

The benefits of offshoring are further substantiated by the Indian call centres that claim they are not only cheaper to run than in the West (40% less), but they are also more productive (one-on-one). This is because the typical call centre worker in India is not only better educated (has a university degree), but the work carries a higher job status. These two factors combine to produce more capable and motivated staff than the less educated and unskilled call centre workers in the West. The Indian call centre worker should therefore be able to offer more value-added services to the customer.

Offshoring also enables customer support work to '*follow the sun*' through the time zones. This allows international companies to offer a 24 hour service even though their employees, in each time zone, are working a normal eight hour day (no night shifts).

4. Problems of Outsourcing and Offshoring

The thought of outsourcing all the company's work and sitting back in your executive chair dreaming of your future strategy may sound like an ideal situation, but outsourcing could introduce a number of new problems as your business moves away from the coalface and you distance yourself from your customers. You may need a shock wake-up call to refocus your attention on the critical aspects of your business.

Consider the following points which could make outsourcing offshore less attractive:

- offshore manufacturers prefer long production runs to achieve an economy of scale - there is a trade-off here with shipping, storage and investment costs
- products may need to be redesigned to simplify the manufacturing, tooling and setting up
- manufacturing in China for instance increases the product turnaround time - if you are in a fast changing market such as 'street fashion', you may not be able to respond quickly enough to fast changing fashion trends
- managing quality in your own company is hard enough, but trying to control quality in a foreign company, in a foreign language, halfway around the world may be impossible - this reinforces the need to simplify the manufacturing process

".... I've got Linda doing the design, Simon is making the product and Dominique is delivering it...."

- certain countries in Asia have been criticized for not respecting copyright and intellectual property rights. To protect your interests you may need to go to the added expense of registering your product with patents and trademarks, and employ agents to look for infringements
- you should always try and keep the link with your end customer - Richard Branson's Virgin empire is very focused on this point. Although the manufacturing of most of Branson's products are outsourced, they all trade under the Virgin logo and brand
- Western customers often find it difficult to understand the foreign accent of the call centre worker even though they have had special elocution training to make their accents sound more American or English
- lines of communication between your business (in the West) and the manufacturer (offshore) are making you totally reliant on telecommunication facilities. Any interruptions or downtime could have a negative impact on your business.

Much of the hype and emotion about outsourcing offshore is over stated. For instance, the US government employment figures show that only 3% of the job layoffs are due to offshoring. This would suggest that perhaps the unions and politicians are overstating the impact on the economy while understating the beneficial source of cheaper consumer products.

Exercises:

1. What work could your business outsource? Discuss the issues.

2. What work could other businesses outsource to your business? What are the mutual benefits?

3. Discuss the problems of controlling quality in an offshore business.

Instructor's Manual: An Instructor's Manual is available with additional exercises and case studies, see <www.knowledgezone.net>.

12
Distribution

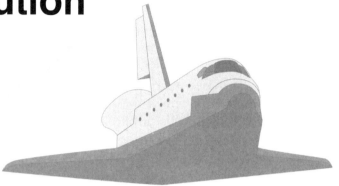

Spotting opportunities, designing and manufacturing new products are one side of the small business entrepreneurs' equation - the other side is determining how to ship and transport the products to the distributors, retailers and customers.

Small companies generally work within a supply chain which has three main components; supply, manufacturing and distribution:

- the supply side focuses on how to supply raw materials and components to the manufacturer
- the manufacturing process draws in the raw materials and components and converts them into sub-assemblies and finished goods - adding value to the products in the process
- the distribution deals with the storage and movement of the finished products to the final customers through a network of distributors, warehouses and retailers.

Your supply chain horizons are from your suppliers in one direction, to your customers in the other direction.

The distribution process was much simpler when everything was made from locally sourced raw materials, manufactured by local labour and available from the corner shop. With globalisation, it is more likely the raw materials and sub-components have been transported half-way round the world to the manufacturers (probably in China), then the finished goods have been shipped back half-way round the world to the customers in the West. With greater shipping distances, greater volumes and longer supply chains, the management of distribution has become an important issue for the small business entrepreneur.

Distribution deals with how to move the products (goods or services) from the manufacturers to the distributors, retailers and customers. Some of the key issues are:

- what kind of distribution channel to use?
- should the product be distributed through a wholesaler?
- should the product be sold through a retailer?
- where should the product or service be available?
- when should the product or service be available?

The answers to these questions obviously depend on the product and the market, and where your company sits in the supply chain.

1. Distribution Channels

Most industries have well established distribution channels for wholesale and retail distribution. One of the popular distribution channels is the hub and spoke arrangement.

Hub and Spoke: The hub and spoke arrangement rationalises the movement of goods within the supply chain. Each hub typically has many feeder spokes (links) to collect and deliver the goods locally. The local goods generally consist of many small items which are collated at the hub into a few large units (usually a container), then shipped hub to hub. At the destination hub the container is unpacked and delivered locally to the spokes.

Although the hub and spoke arrangement appears to double the handling and movement of goods locally, it does rationalise and reduce the number of movements between the hubs.

The postal service uses the hub and spoke arrangement, where they collect the mail from many local post boxes and deliver them to the nearest main hub. At the main hub, the mail is sorted and shipped out to other hubs where it is sorted and delivered to the local sub-post offices, and then delivered to your letter box.

The airline industry is another example of a hub and spoke arrangement. For instance, if you wanted to fly between Southampton and the Kruger National Park, you would need to fly on a local flight from Southampton to Heathrow, then internationally from Heathrow to Johannesburg (hub to hub), then take a local flight from Johannesburg to the Kruger National Park.

The opportunities for the small business entrepreneur are often found in the local niche markets - this could be local deliveries, or local flights between provincial airports.

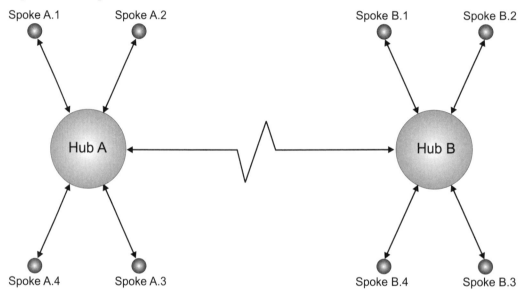

Figure 12.1: Hub and Spoke Arrangement - showing two airport hubs and many local spokes.

2. Selling Direct to the Customer

Many small manufacturing companies have expanded vertically along the supply chain so that they can offer their products direct to their customers. This essentially cuts out the middleman (distributors and retailers), enabling the manufacturers to offer competitive prices yet maintain their profit margins.

Ordering products through the Internet cuts out even more of the human involvement in the supply chain. The ultimate is the fully automated B2B system where the customer places the order on the Internet, and the rest of the process is automatic.

B2B (business-to-business) and B2C (business-to-customer) procurement platforms are business facilities offered through the Internet. At their simplest, B2B market places are just on-line catalogues. Sellers list their products with

prices, specifications and delivery terms. Buyers browse the catalogues on-line, place their orders and make payments electronically. This is exactly how <www.amazon.com> sells books, and how <www.dell.com> sell their computers.

The potential benefits for buyers include dramatically reduced procurement administration costs, reduced delivery times, lower material prices, and faster supply chains. The benefits for the sellers include increased sales volume, lower cost of making a sale, and reduced inventory requirements.

Web sites are a great opportunity for the small business entrepreneur, because they are relatively inexpensive to set up and host, yet they can make the entrepreneur appear to be a large established company even though they might be operating from their spare room. And, when the sales kick-in, this could be another dot com company in the making.

B2B procurement, therefore, offers the small business entrepreneur the opportunity to;

- reduce transaction costs
- generate less paperwork
- provide an economy of scale through consolidated purchasing
- reduce the level of unapproved 'rogue' purchases.

The small business entrepreneur also needs to be aware of the associated risks of the global market, because working through the Internet will encourage the entrepreneur to look for the best deals world wide. If this leads to outsourcing to manufacturers offshore this will add more links to the supply chain and longer lead times to manage.

Michael Dell: Michael Dell is an excellent example of someone who has used the Internet and B2B procurement to gain competitive advantage. Dell started his computer business from his dormitory room at the University of Texas. He was a whiz kid who focused on building better computers and selling them directly to the customer for less than the established computer manufacturer's price. Dell's entrepreneurial approach integrates manufacturing with the demand, by building the computers to order. Dell further cuts out the middleman, with broad based advertising encouraging the customer to contact them directly through B2B (business-to-business) and B2C (business-to-customer) procurement. Dell has been a key player in pioneering this paradigm shift in supply chain management and B2B procurement.

3. Warehousing

Warehousing is an important part of the supply chain and distribution process. Warehousing typically involves checking the goods into the warehouse, handling, storage and dispatch.

Receiving Goods: The receiving function cross-checks the delivery note against the delivered goods. The back-office will later cross-check the delivery note against the purchase order.

Quality Control: Where possible, the quality of a product is checked against the required condition and specification.

Handling Equipment: Some deliveries may require special handling equipment. Most goods these days are packed on to pallets, shrink wrapped and placed in containers. A small business might require a fork-lift truck to move the pallets out of the containers and stack them in its warehouse.

Special Storage Conditions: Some deliveries could require special storage conditions, perishable goods for example might need to be refrigerated.

Stock Control: Packing goods away neatly is one thing, but finding them again is another – this is where the entrepreneur needs effective inventory management skills. Inventory management logs all goods into the system and notes their location and quantity, so when you need to retrieve them you know exactly where they are. Stock control also documents how many items are in the warehouse and flags the minimum stock level for reordering (MRP, Material Requirement Planning). Book shops are a good example, when a book is sold it is automatically reordered.

Dispatch: The dispatch function fulfils the customer's order, packs the product and delivers it to the customer.

4. Trade-Offs

Cheaper manufacturing costs in Asia, in general, and China in particular, are forcing companies to outsource and offshore their manufacturing to remain competitive. This is creating a number of trade-offs that need to be considered:
- reduced manufacturing costs
- less product flexibility
- increased shipping costs
- increased storage costs
- longer lead times.

The initial attraction to outsource the manufacturing offshore is to reduce the manufacturing costs, but this needs to be balanced with a number of other considerations.

Manufacturing Costs: High volume, long production runs in the East are offering much lower rates than the West.

Increased Shipping Costs: Moving the manufacturing to Asia from your home base will increase the shipping costs.

Increased Storage Costs: Although increasing the production run will reduce the unit cost, you need to balance this with increased handling and storage costs at the other end of the supply chain.

Longer Lead Times: The physical distance of Asia from the markets in the West could cause unacceptable production lead times. Air freight is the fastest option, but this might be too expensive for low value goods.

Longer lead times increase the just-in-time (JIT) procurement allowance. Companies need to maintain a certain stock level to ensure they can always supply the customer. There is another trade-off here between customer service (or product availability) and level of inventory. The level of inventory is a function of the confidence you have in the sales figures and the risk of losing customers if you cannot supply timeously. To address these concerns you may need to increase the stock levels which will increase the storage costs and money tied up in stock.

Inflexible: Many factories in the East specialise in long production runs of the same item, for example, there is an enormous factory in China that only manufactures socks – 20% of the world's supply! And another enormous factory in a neighbouring city that only produces gloves. These factories can mass produce items very cheaply, but are not flexible enough to accommodate short high quality production runs. This is evident in the fashion industry where basic garments are mass produced in the East, but the short run, high couture garments are made in the West.

	Advantages	Disadvantages
Costs	Lower manufacturing costs	Higher shipping costs
Long production runs	Lower manufacturing costs	High storage costs
Delivery time		Long lead times
Long lead time		Higher inventory costs

Figure 12.2: Summary of Offshore Manufacturing Trade-offs

Exercises:

1. Where does your company sit in the supply chain?

2. What distribution arrangement do you use? Discuss how you could use a hub and spoke arrangement, and B2B direct distribution.

3. Discuss the trade-offs you have made between where to manufacture, shipping, inventory levels and customer service.

13
Financial Statements

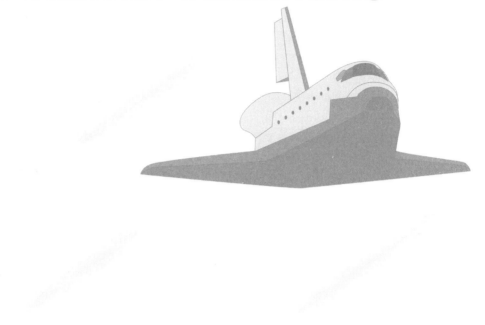

In the past the typical entrepreneur might have started with an ad hoc **shoe-box accounting** system which he kept under the bed - but times have changed. Today the proactive entrepreneur is far more likely to start with a visit to an accountant and a bank manager so that he can obtain sufficient funds to hit the ground running.

It is in the entrepreneur's interests to start the financial process with a visit to an accountant, because they have the business experience and software to quickly develop a cashflow forecast for the entrepreneur's new venture or business proposal. The entrepreneur can then take this cashflow forecast as part of his business plan to the bank manager and request funds.

In the highly dynamic and competitive small business market, business opportunities do not last for long. The entrepreneur intuitively knows he has to capitalise on his innovative ideas and get his product to market before the competition. To do this the entrepreneur usually needs outside finance - and where better to start than the local bank!

Presenting a bank manager with a cashflow forecast shows them you have done your homework and have the basis of a viable and credible business plan. If you are going the franchise route, for example, the franchisor would provide this financial information.

The next challenge is to develop an accounting system to manage the business accounts. Accurate accounting records are essential to keep your finger on the financial pulse of your business and to comply with tax and other statutory reporting requirements.

Estimating techniques, business plans, accounting procedures and sources of finance all come together to give an overall picture of the company's financial performance and forecast for the future. Most companies (if not all) are in business to make a profit, so monitoring financial performance is important, particularly if investment and set up costs have a negative impact on the cashflow. Even 'not for profit' organisations providing social services, need to balance their books to stay in operation.

The reason there is a confusingly large number of accounting statements is because each statement presents a different view of the company's financial situation and performance. If you only look at one statement, you may be unwittingly misleading yourself to believe your company is doing well while, the company may in fact be one step away from bankruptcy. For example, the company could be making a healthy profit according to the trading profit and loss account, but have negative cashflow in their bank account because of stocking costs and late payments from customers.

As a first step, the small business accounts can be subdivided into two distinct areas (see figure 13.1):

- **project accounts** for setting up a new venture
- **business accounts** for the day-to-day operation of the business.

All companies need to compile business accounts to manage the company on a day-to-day basis, but for new ventures and significant changes, the entrepreneur (project manager) needs a set of project accounts to plan and control the transition period.

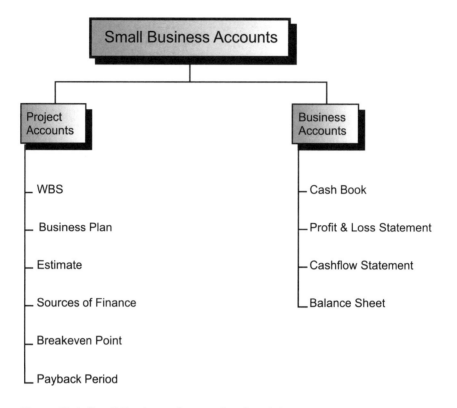

Figure 13.1: Small Business Accounting Breakdown

1. Project Accounts

There are a number of special project management tools and techniques which the entrepreneur (project manager) can use to plan and control their projects. Project accounts focus on direct costing and use a number of documents to plan and control the project's progress. Consider the following:

- WBS (Work Breakdown Structure)
- Business plan (Feasibility Study)
- Estimate
- Sources of finance
- Breakeven point analysis
- Payback period.

WBS: The work breakdown structure subdivides the scope of work into manageable chunks of work (work packages) which are easier and more accurate to estimate (top down and bottom up). The work packages can then be assigned to a department or a person for execution.

Business Plan: As ideas and opportunities evolve into marketable products, at some point you need to formalise your approach with a coherent business plan that encapsulates short and long term estimates on paper. The business plan should not only ensure the small business is feasible, but also confirm there is a market for the product, and that the new venture is making the best use of your time and resources (see the chapter on *Business Plans* for more information).

Estimate: Accurate estimating is essential to underpin the small business entrepreneur's ability to plan and control the work. If the company tenders for work, then accurate estimating is even more important, because you will be committing your company contractually based on the estimate (see the chapter on *Estimating* for more information).

Sources of Finance: Ready cash and seed money are the life-blood of the entrepreneur's start up ventures. Without sufficient funds the new venture's success will be self-limited. There will simply not be funds and resources available to develop the product and build-up stock until the positive cashflow kicks-in. The chapter on *Sources of Finance* in my book *Entrepreneurs Toolkit* discusses a number of funding options.

Breakeven Point Analysis: The breakeven point is the number of products the company needs to sell to cover all the set up costs, after that the venture starts making a profit (see the chapter on *Breakeven Point* for more information).

Payback Period: The payback period is the time it takes to reach the breakeven point. This gives a measure of the time the company is exposed to the risk of the market changing (see the chapter on *Breakeven Point* for more information).

2. Business Accounts

Businesses need to keep track of all their day to day transactions in order to be able to produce meaningful accounting statements on a periodic basis (monthly, quarterly or annually).

Day to day accounting usually utilises a Cash Book system which can be either manual or computerised. There are a number of off the shelf software packages available (see the chapter on *Cash Book* for more information). The main accounting statements to consider are:

- Cash Book
- Trading Account
- Profit and Loss Account (statement of financial performance)
- Cashflow Statement
- Balance Sheet (statement of financial position).

Cash Book: The cash book collates all the company's financial transactions (see the chapter on *Cash Book* for more information).

Trading Account: The trading account calculates all the incurred expenses to make the product, and all the income from selling the product - the bottom line gives the gross profit or loss for the period. If there are a number of ventures, each has a separate trading account to arrive at the total gross profit.

Profit and Loss Account: The statement of financial performance takes the total gross profit and loss from the trading account, deducts the overhead costs (i.e. those costs which cannot be directly apportioned to the product) and adds any other non-operating income (e.g. bank interest) to arrive at the net profit or loss for the period.

Cashflow Statement: The cashflow forecast quantifies the flow of money (cash) in and out of the business (usually through your bank account). The time frame is typically monthly to coincide with the normal business accounting period.

To appreciate the difference between the profit and loss statement and the cashflow statement you need to understand the difference between incurred or committed costs, and actual costs (see the chapter on *Cashflow Statements* for a discussion on cash method and accrual method).

Balance Sheet: The balance sheet, also called statement of financial position, is a snapshot of the balance between the company's assets and the company's liabilities on any particular day. For management purposes the balance sheet can be presented in a two column format of assets and liabilities (figure 18.4), or as a one column format with the figures from previous years to show the trends (figure 18.5) (see the chapter on *Cash Books* for more information).

Exercises:

1. Explain the difference between project accounting and business accounting. What statements would you use to plan and control the finances of a project or new venture?

2. What statements would you use to plan and control the finances of a small company?

3. What small business software packages are available in your area?

Instructor's Manual: An Instructor's Manual is available with additional exercises and case studies, see <www.knowledgezone.net>.

14
Business Plans

As ideas and opportunities evolve into marketable products, at some point the small business entrepreneur needs to formalise his approach with a coherent business plan. The business plan should not only ensure that the small business is feasible, but also confirm there is a market for the product, and that the venture is making the best use of the entrepreneur's time and resources. The bottom line is that the business plan must set out the entrepreneur's goals and how the entrepreneur plans to achieve them.

Business start up enthusiasm and workload can easily sideline the need for a business plan. Research in America suggests that only a third of business start ups actually develop a business plan. Bill Gates and Paul Allen, for example, did not develop one when they started Microsoft in 1975! In their defence, if they had tried to do a competitive analysis or a customer analysis at the time, they would not have known who their competitors or customers were, or have been able to make the classic comparison of strengths and weaknesses with respect to their competition.

The business plan (also called **feasibility study** in project management terminology) is an all encompassing approach which identifies the business, the product, the market, the business feasibility and its financial requirements. The business plan includes a number of accounting statements which help to quantify the situation, together with a plan for dealing with all the potential problems the new venture might encounter. But most importantly the business plan should address the venture's three main considerations:

- confirm the product can be produced
- confirm the product has a market
- confirm the investors can make a return on their investment.

The business plan is a frequently misunderstood document. Many people think it is only used to raise finance (for which it is a key document), but consider these other uses;

- preparing a business plan forces the entrepreneur to take an objective, critical and unemotional look at the business concept and confirm that all aspects of the idea and opportunity are working together
- the business plan is an operating model which outlines a plan of action for execution and control
- the business plan establishes a business framework to guide the venture and help make decisions in the future
- the business plan instils confidence in the small business team's abilities to manage the venture
- the business plan shows there is a market for the product
- the business plan helps to communicate the purpose of the venture to the stakeholders.

The business plan is presented here as a key document which pulls together a number of inter-related management topics into one integrated document.

Whichever finance and market research route the entrepreneur takes, even if he finances the venture out of personal savings, he should produce a business plan to ensure the funds are not being put into an unacceptable risk. Most entrepreneurs would consider that writing an elaborate business plan just to convince the bank manager they are worthy of a loan as a complete waste of time. To persuade an entrepreneur to develop a business plan, means the entrepreneur must be able to produce one quickly and easily, and the output must be meaningful and obviously beneficial.

If the entrepreneur is unsure how to develop a business, this is the time to consider seeking a **mentor** who will help collate and present the entrepreneur's creative ideas into a coherent business plan.

1. Business Plan Structure

The business plan structure includes a number of sections which outline what the entrepreneur intends to do with respect to what, when, how and why. Business plans tend to follow a standard format that give a clear overview of a new venture in a format that bank managers prefer.

Executive Summary:
- overviews the new venture
- outlines the type of business
- identifies the market
- outlines the business potential and sales forecast
- estimates a profit forecast
- estimates how much money needs to be raised
- calculates the return on investment
- assesses the risk.

Business Description of the Product:
- describes what the product or service offers
- identifies what is different or unique about the product or service
- briefly outlines the competition
- explains how the product will be developed, and what new products are in the pipeline
- lists what patents have been applied for.

Organisation Structure:
- presents an organisation structure and management plan
- lists past employment and business experience
- includes a CV for each team member
- lists strengths and weaknesses
- identifies stakeholders, particularly close links with suppliers and contractors.

Sales and Marketing:

- outlines likely customer profiles
- estimates market size, growth (past, present, future)
- identifies niche market opportunities
- identifies competitors: who they are, their size, market share, possible responses to the product, and price strategy
- explains how the product will be sold and distributed; Internet, direct mail, tele-sales, distributors, retailers
- outlines promotions, advertising, sales brochures.

Manufacturing and Distribution:

- describes location
- lists equipment and manufacturing facilities
- outlines build-method and feasibility study
- lists suppliers
- describes warehousing and stock control (JIT)
- outlines distribution system
- outlines shipping, transport and vehicles.

Financial Statement:

- estimates the set up costs
- estimates the operational costs
- forecasts sales
- determines the breakeven point
- determines the payback period
- produces a cashflow statement
- estimates the return on investment (ROI) and discounted cashflow
- identifies the sources of finance.

Risk Management:

- discusses risk analysis
- discusses risk response
- discusses disaster recovery.

".... reach for the perfect business plan - the holy grail.... "

2. Executive Summary

It is accepted practice to start a business plan with an executive summary to give a brief overview of the new venture. The executive summary should get straight to the point and only focus on the key issues and the bottom line. This enables the reader (potential investor) to quickly get a feel for the new venture without having to plough through the whole business plan.

Start the business plan with an overview of the type of business, its structure and its strategy. Give brief details of the product or service and confirm the business can manufacture and deliver the product to the potential customers.

Confirm there is a market for the product - this may be supported by market research. Give some details of potential sales, market growth and competition. Outline how the product will be promoted and advertised to create awareness and establish the brand image.

Provide brief financial statements giving; cost breakdown, income breakdown, breakeven point analysis, payback period and a forecast profit and loss statement. Develop a cashflow forecast to outline the borrowing requirement, how much money is needed, and when the investors can expect to be paid back, together with a forecast return on their investment (ROI). Outline the risk assessment of the venture and identify the main risks and the likely responses.

3. Business Description

The business description outlines the business concept and strategy. This is where you need to specify the type of industry and the market in broad terms.

- what product (goods or service) is being offered and who are the target customers
- outline where the company sits in the supply chain, and explain how the product will be manufactured and distributed
- list what support services are required including suppliers, contractors, advertising, promotions and customer service strategies.

State the main operations of the business in terms of its current and proposed business activities. Indicate what the objectives of the business will be in the short term (1 year), medium term (2-3 years) and long term (3+ years). Describe the product in terms of competitive and technological advantage (unique features), any legal protection enjoyed (such as copyright, patents and trademarks), as well as planned expansion with future products (MK11, sequels and series).

If you own the premises, state the present valuation and age of the building(s). If the premises are leased, give details of the lease (period, rental, option to renew).

Give details of the floor area and scope for expansion and the suitability of the premises for the proposed type of business.

Name the local authority and other governing bodies, and the official approvals that are required for the operation of the business. Comment on the suitability of the location, particularly in the case of retail businesses where the customers come to you. Use the following headings as guidelines; visibility, size, image, accessibility to target markets, vehicles (parking) and pedestrian traffic flow, together with future growth and development in the area which may influence the business.

4. Organisation Structure

Introduce the business with a brief history of why and how it was originally formed. Provide details of its legal identity and registration – this would typically be a sole trader, partnership, franchise or a limited company.

Identify all the key people, as people are an organisation's most valuable asset. The management plan should identify the entrepreneur, the project team, the management organisation structure, the proposed suppliers and sub-contractors (see figure 14.1 below). CVs should be supplied for all the key roles, outlining qualifications, appropriate work experience and knowledge of the industry, together with any other special attributes.

Mention the extent to which the venture will create local employment, especially if the business funding is influenced by job creation schemes and government grants. This should also include external employment of sub-contractors, suppliers, professional support and other stakeholders.

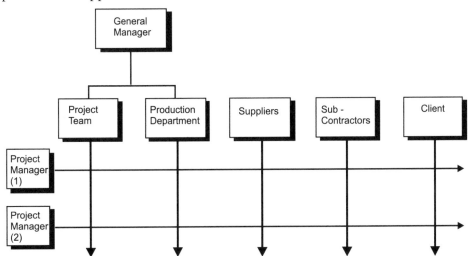

Figure 14.1: Matrix Organisation Structure - showing how the entrepreneur (project manager) interfaces with the project team, the production department, suppliers, sub-contractors and the client

5. Sales and Marketing

The marketing section should confirm there is a market for the product or service and this should be supported where possible by tangible market research. This is the section in which the target customer's profile should be discussed, so the reader can visualise the customers putting their hands in their pockets and buying the products – who, when, where and for how much.

Estimate the **size of the market** and its future **growth potential**. This could be local, national and, increasingly, international through the global Internet.

Assess the **competition** and suggest why someone would buy your product in preference to the competitors'. Estimate your share of the market; note here if your product is for a niche market or general market. Based on the above information, estimate the future sales figures over the next three years. Identify your competitors, their size, market share and possible response to your product and price strategy.

Outline the price strategy, relating to the identified competition. This is the place to comment on penetration price and price skimming if appropriate.

Comment on how the **advertising** and promotion of the product will reach the target market. This could be broad based advertising to a wide market, or direct promotions to a niche market.

Comment on how **customer service** will respond to customer enquiries and problems. Friendly customer service is essential to ensure customers are dealt with quickly and efficiently. It is also the best way to ensure repeat business, which in turn should reduce future marketing costs.

".... buy one get two free .... "

6. Manufacturing and Distribution

The manufacturing section describes how the product is made, detailing the critical elements of the manufacturing process. It details the build-method and confirms what special equipment and expertise are required, together with their availability. It also highlights to what extent the company has production advantage over the competitors. For example, automated production lines might give an economy of scale which lowers the unit cost.

This is the section to discuss whether the company plans to outsource and offshore its work as a means to gain competitive advantage.

This is also the section to explain what is involved in making and delivering the product or service by outlining;

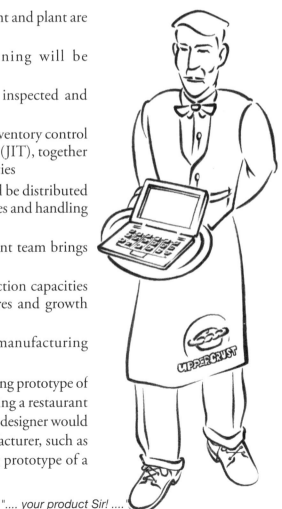

- how the product or service is designed
- what raw materials are used, who the main suppliers are, and what credit terms are enjoyed
- what manufacturing equipment and plant are required
- how the production planning will be managed
- how quality will be assured, inspected and controlled
- the proposed holding stock, inventory control system, and delivery lead time (JIT), together with any special storage facilities
- how the product or service will be distributed and delivered, and what vehicles and handling equipment are required
- the experience the management team brings to the manufacturing process
- the present and future production capacities relating this to the sales figures and growth projections
- the risk assessment of the manufacturing process.

Now is the time to demonstrate a working prototype of the product. For example, a chef opening a restaurant would produce sample meals, a fashion designer would present a clothing range, and a manufacturer, such as Dyson, would demonstrate a working prototype of a domestic cleaner.

".... your product Sir! ...."

7. Financial Statement

The financial statement is primarily concerned with forecasts of profitability and financial liability. For banks and venture capital firms thinking of investing in a new venture, the financial statement is one of the key sections (together with growth potential of course). You need to clearly demonstrate that you have a sound financial plan which you can manage and control.

Estimate and collate all the costs involved in setting up the new venture, and all the operational costs to make the product or service. The estimate should list all the items that need to be purchased, and their costs and means of payment (credit, lease etc.). The estimate should then calculate budgets for:

- the start up budget required to launch the new venture or product
- the operational budget to cover the first 12 months of production, or until positive cashflow kicks in
- the premises (mortgage or rent payments)
- the capital equipment (hire purchase or lease payments).

Use the forecast **profit and loss statement** to show how the new venture will make a trading profit, and use the **cashflow forecast** to give monthly snap shots of the bank balance and the need for short term finance. The cashflow forecast should also include proposed funding and repayments (over an extended period of two or three years), and property loans over ten years.

Use the **breakeven point** analysis to assess the financial risk by quantifying the number of sales required to cover the set up costs, and use the **payback period** to quantify the time to reach the breakeven point (see *Breakeven Point* chapter for calculations).

The financial statement should list all the other financial documents that the company will produce and the frequency. The key documents should include:

- sources of finance and repayment schedule (see *Entrepreneurs Toolkit* for more information)
- cash book (lists all the incomes and expenses)
- balance sheet (lists all the assets and liabilities).

8. Risk Management

The risk management statement should identify all the potential risks that could prevent the new venture reaching its objectives and how you propose to respond to the risks. This could be to eliminate, mitigate, deflect or accept the risks. If you are accepting the risks, this is the place to outline your contingencies.

This is the section to outline what **disaster recovery** measures will be put in place to respond to the ultimate risks. This should particularly indicate how you will ensure the business will be able to continue operating in the event of a disaster, and how the data and information will be backed-up and recovered.

Business Plan: Developing a realistic business plan could help prevent the entrepreneur pursuing a new venture that is doomed to fail. If a new venture is marginal at best, the business plan should show where and why the venture is questionable.

More than half of all new businesses fail within the first three years - lack of business management planning has been identified as a major cause of this failure. A good business plan is therefore essential to help pinpoint unrealistic marketing, unforeseen competition, and unforeseen problems.

The business plan is the flip side of innovation and opportunity. Without innovation and creative ideas there is no small business venture to consider, but conversely without a sensible business plan there may be no more ventures, because the entrepreneur may have sunk all his funds into a white elephant.

Exercises:

Write a business plan for one of the following new ventures;
1. A fashion retail outlet in London's fashionable Bond Street.
2. A web design business in Hong Kong offering B2B procurement facilities.
3. A restaurant in Cape Town providing business lunches.

Instructor's Manual: An Instructor's Manual is available with additional exercises and case studies, see <www.knowledgezone.net>.

15
Estimating Techniques

For small business entrepreneurs to plan and control their work effectively, accurate estimating is essential. If their company tenders for work, then accurate estimating is even more important, because now they will be committing their company contractually, based on the estimate.

The accuracy of the estimate is usually dependent on the amount of information available and the amount of time available to produce the estimate - both of these are often in short supply. With more time available, the accuracy of information and the accuracy of the estimate should increase but, in the commercial world, contractors usually have little time to quote. It is therefore essential to develop a number of estimating techniques which can produce estimates quickly and accurately. Estimates can be subdivided into three basic types which relate to the level of detail and the level of accuracy:

- concept estimate
- business plan
- costing.

Concept Estimate: Is an initial filter to select which ventures warrant further investigation. The concept estimate could be produced very quickly (may be over a beer!) based on a limited scope of work using scale factors to give a low level of accuracy +/-25%. For example, the cost of building a house may be estimated as $X per square metre of floor area.

Business Plan: The business plan includes a detailed estimate which confirms the new venture is financially feasible and will make a return on the entrepreneur's investment. With more detailed information and more time, the business plan should give a level of accuracy of +/- 10%.

Costing: Costing is the most accurate estimate based on a complete scope of work, complete set of drawings, and a complete set of plans - in other words everything is known. Compiling all the information will take time, but the level of accuracy should increase to +/- 1%.

1. Direct Costs

Before outlining a few estimating techniques, it is important to understand how the costs are subdivided into a number of categories (direct cost, indirect costs etc.). Direct costs, as the term implies, are costs which can be specifically identified and assigned to a job. This means direct costs can be individually budgeted and controlled. Consider the following;

- direct management costs refer to the entrepreneur (project manager) and other managers working on the new venture
- direct labour costs refer to the people working on an activity
- direct material costs refer to the material used to complete an activity
- direct equipment costs refer to the cost of using machinery and plant to complete an activity
- direct bought-in expenses refer to the costs associated with services used directly to complete an activity.

2. Indirect Costs

Indirect costs are overhead type costs which cannot be directly attributed to any particular job, but are required to keep the company functioning. Indirect costs are usually financed by an overhead recovery charge which is generally included in the labour rate. Consider the following:

- indirect management costs refer to head office staff
- indirect labour costs refer to reception, maintenance and security functions required to keep the company running
- indirect material costs refer to stationary, cleaning materials, maintenance parts, etc.
- indirect equipment costs include costs associated with computers, etc.
- other indirect costs include training, insurance, etc.

3. Labour Costs

Labour costs are a key component of most jobs, and are generally expressed as so much per hour, or a fixed cost based on an estimated number of hours. This section will explain how to determine the labour charge-out rate for your company. The labour costs considered here are for the workforce and are therefore a direct cost. Although the salaries of your workforce may be clearly identified, there are also a number of other associated costs which form part of the labour rate. The labour rate is calculated by aggregating the various costs and dividing them by the number of manhours worked. This process is explained in the following worked example. Here the costs have been subdivided into four main headings:

    A. employee's salary
    B. employee's associated labour costs
    C. employee's contribution to overheads
    D. employee's contribution to company profit.

		Cost per month	Days lost per month
A.	Salary	$3000	
B. 1	Medical insurance	$200	
B. 2	Sickness benefit		1
B. 3	Annual holiday		1
B. 4	Training courses	$100	1
B. 5	Protective clothing	$50	
B. 6	Car allowance	$500	
B. 7	Housing allowance	$100	
B. 8	Subsistence allowance	$100	
B. 9	Pension	$250	
B. 10	Tool allowance	$100	
B. 11	Productivity bonus	$100	
B. 12	Standing time		1
B. 13	Inclement weather		1
	Total associated labour costs	**$1500**	5
C.	Contribution to overheads 30% of employee's salary	$900	
D.	Company profit 33% of employee's salary	$1000	

Figure 15.1: Labour Costs

Labour rate $= \dfrac{\text{Total monthly costs (A + B + C + D)}}{\text{Total number of normal working hours per month}}$

Where the average working month is 21 days, the average days lost per month are 5 days and eight hours are worked per day.

Labour rate $= \dfrac{3000+1500+900+1000}{(21-5) \times 8}$

$= \$ 50/ \text{hr}.$

Some of the above items may be difficult to quantify without access to statistical analysis, for example, days lost due to sickness and standing time. They should, however, be recognised as potential costs and a figure assigned if only as a contribution to an unknown amount. The end product of this analysis should be a labour rate per hour.

Overtime: This brings us to an interesting question. Based on the above calculations, how do we cost out overtime? If all the associated labour costs have been covered by the employee's contribution during normal working hours, can one assume they do not need to be paid for again? If yes, then you need only assign costs to the following headings:

- A. labour wages overtime rate (assume double time)
- B. employee's associated labour costs (assume zero)
- C. employee's contribution to indirect variable costs (the same at $900)
- D. employee's contribution to company profit (the same at $1000)

One can also assume there will be no lost time, because the employee is either working overtime or not.

Labour rate (overtime) $= \dfrac{6000 + 0 + 900 + 1000}{21 \times 8} = \$47/\text{hr}$

So the overtime rate is actually less than the normal rate! However, in industry and commerce the overtime rate to the client usually increases as a multiple of the employee overtime rate (time and a half, or double time).

As a rule of thumb, the labour rate can be calculated approximately from the worker's wages (which are known). The expenses can be factored into thirds as below:

- 1/3 labour wages
- 1/3 contribution to overheads
- 1/3 company profit.

An even easier way is to see what other companies are charging! You will have to do this anyway to ensure your rates are competitive.

4. Procurement Costs

This section will determine the costs to procure all the bought-in goods and services. The simplest method is to add a percentage to the buying price to cover all the procurement costs as an indirect cost. Consider the following table:

Department	Scope of Work	Costs
Drawing office	Bill of materials, specifications	1000
Buying office	Source suppliers and vendors	300
Quality department	Prequalify suppliers	200
Buying office	Tender cycle, adjudication and selection	500
Planning office	Procurement schedule	500
Buying office	Place order, expedite	200
Quality department	Goods inwards inspection	100
Warehouse	Material handling, inventory and stock control	1000
Accounts department	Pay invoices	200
Shareholders	Profit	800
Total Costs		**4800**

Figure 15.2: Procurement Costs

$$\text{Procurement percentage} = \frac{\text{Procurement costs}}{\text{Total cost of materials}} \times 100$$

For example, if the total cost of the procured items is $50,000 and the cost of procurement is $4,800 as per figure 15.2, then the percentage will be as below:

$$\frac{\$4,800}{\$50,000} \times 100 = 9.6\%$$

Some of the above costs may be covered by another budget, for example, the inspection and pre-qualifying of suppliers could fall under the QA budget; in which case, they should not be included here (double accounting). The procurement costs would generally be developed at the company level and apply to all the company's projects. Typical percentages would be between 10% to 20%.

5. Time Related Costs

Time related costs are those costs which change as the duration of the venture changes. As the time to set up a new venture is extended or shortened, some costs will increase, while others will reduce. The purpose of the time/cost trade-off analysis is to show the overall impact on the budget.

For example, if setting up a venture is extended by two months, then all the rent and insurance type costs which are paid on a monthly basis will increase. And conversely, if the setting up of the venture is shortened by two months, all the time related costs will reduce. But, there is an interesting trade-off with labour costs - if you reduce the duration of the venture then the labour force will have to work overtime or do shift work which will actually **increase** the labour costs.

To gauge the overall impact of changing the duration of a venture, the costs that change need to be set up on a spreadsheet so that you can look at the bottom line.

6. Unit Rates

Although new ventures tend to be a unique undertaking, many of the tasks are similar to previous jobs. It is, therefore, expedient to use unit rates for common items of work based on previous performance. This technique estimates a job's cost from an empirically developed book of unit rates. For example, consider the following parameters in the table below:

Unit	Description
Per linear metre	Pipe work, wiring, welding
Per square metre	House building, decorating, painting
Per cubic metre	Concrete, water supply
Per tonne	Ship building, cargo freight
Per HP, KW	Generator power, electrical supply
Per mile, Km	Car hire, transport
Per hour	Labour rate, plant hire

Figure 15.3: Unit Rates

Unit rates are probably the most commonly used estimating technique and will form the basis of most estimates because they are easy to measure and easy to budget. Even fixed priced contracts usually contain a unit price clause for charging out additional work.

7. Factoring

The factoring technique relates certain costs to a percentage of a known cost. For example, the management fee for a contract could be estimated at 5% of the contract price. Therefore, when the contract price is established the factoring technique adds 5% to cover the management costs. For example, if the contract price is $1,000,000 the management fee will be an additional 5%, which is $50,000.

	Factor
Management fee	5 % of contract price
Quality assurance	1% of contract price
Machine foundations	2% of machine price
Pipework	20% of generator price
Consumables	10% of material price
Profit	20% of construction price

Figure 15.4: Factoring

When the core costs of the new venture have been established, the associated ratios can be calculated very quickly. These ratios should be confirmed progressively from the closeout reports of previous jobs.

8. Estimating Format

The final estimate (quotation) is a compilation of figures from many different sources (see figure 15.5). The left hand column quantifies the scope of work, which can be subdivided as a work breakdown structure (WBS), or as a list of jobs. The WBS helps to ensure all the items of work are included in the list.

Each job can be further subdivided into labour, material, equipment and transport. By setting up the estimate on a spreadsheet, the amounts can be added horizontally and vertically to give the total cost per job, the total cost for all the labour, material, equipment and transport, and the total cost of the new venture.

Scope of Work (WBS)	Labour	Material	Equipment	Transport	Total Costs
Task 1	100	50			150
Task 2	200		100	50	350
Task 3	100				100
Task 4	150	50	50	50	300
Task 5	100		200		300
Total Cost	650	100	350	100	1200

Figure 15.5: Estimating Format

Contingency: Do you build in a contingency amount into the labour rate or do you add it on as a separate item? This partly depends on your client. Some clients may be surprised to be charged a contingency against risk - in which case you should build it into the labour rate. Other clients might want to see that you have budgeted for a contingency cost - in which case show the contingency cost separately.

A final important word on estimating - your current venture can provide valuable estimating information for your future ventures, therefore, it is essential to keep a project log book. Entrepreneurs who do not analyse the performance of their previous ventures are condemned to repeat their history of poor estimates and cost overruns.

Exercises:

1. The concept estimate needs to be calculated very quickly - what methods would you use for your new ventures?

2. Calculate the labour cost for your company.

3. Outline what items of work on your projects can be subdivided into unit costs.

Instructor's Manual: An Instructor's Manual is available with additional exercises and case studies, see <www.knowledgezone.net>.

16
Cashflow Statements

The financial success of a new venture depends not only on the product making a profit, but also being able to finance the business through the start up and survival phases. Statistics clearly indicate that more companies go into liquidation because of cashflow problems than for any other reason. The small business entrepreneur must therefore closely plan and control the company's cashflow. There are two basic ways of managing small business accounts, these are the cash method and the accrual method.

Cash Method. The cash method of accounting only records income when you receive the cash from your customers and, likewise, only records expenses when you pay a supplier. Most individuals use the cash method for their personal finances because it is the simplest and the least time-consuming. However, this method can distort the bottom line if you offer credit to your customers and if you buy on credit from your suppliers.

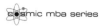

Accrual Method. The accrual method records income when the sale occurs or when an item is ordered. It does not wait until the product or service is delivered, or when the customers actually pay. Likewise, the expenses are recorded when the goods or services are ordered, even though you might pay for them later.

The accrual method gives a more accurate picture of the financial situation than the cash method. This is because the incomes are recorded on the books when they are actually earned and the expenses are recorded when they are actually ordered or incurred. This enables income earned in a period to be compared directly with the expenses incurred in that same period to derive the income.

Of the two methods, the cash method of accounting is easier to maintain compared to the accrual method because income is only recorded when you receive the cash and expenses are only recorded when the cash is paid. With the accrual method there may be twice as many transactions.

Many businesses keep their accounts on a cash basis and then provide their accountants with the end of year figures for accounts receivable, accounts payable and stock. The accountant compiles the extra bookkeeping to produce the annual accounts. These are often prepared some months after the year end, so the feedback is somewhat historical.

While the cash method is simpler to compile, it is really only suitable for small businesses with a small amount of transactions. As small businesses expand they need to move their accounts to an accruals basis so that they are aware of the amount owed and owing at the end of each accounting period. This is where accounting packages for the small business come into their own.

".... your can't have too much cash ...."

1. Cashflow Forecast

The cashflow forecast quantifies the flow of money (cash) in and out of the business (usually through a bank account). The time frame is typically monthly to coincide with the normal business accounting period. The cashflow forecast is generally presented over a number of months as a mix of estimated and actual figures. The cashflow forecast generally starts as an estimate for the next 12 months, but as timenow moves forward, so the estimated figures are updated with actual figures. And even the estimated figures may be revised based on the current information and trends.

The cashflow forecast lends itself to be set up on a computerised spreadsheet or database format which calculates and updates the figures automatically. This forecast will not only allow you to monitor the bottom line (closing balance), but also to simulate the figures to identify areas of risk.

The example below (figure 16.1) shows how the cashflow for work carried out in March can be spread over a few months - before and after March.

	Timing	Jan	Feb	Mar	Apr	May	Jun
Opening balance							
Income	1 month credit				9000		
Cost of Sales							
Rent	1 month up front		1000				
Heating, light, water	1 month credit				200		
Tel, Internet	1 month credit				100		
Professional fees	2 months credit					100	
Bank charges	1 month credit				100		
Wages	paid in the month the work carried out			5000			
Material	1 month credit				2000		
Equipment	2 months up front	300					
Transport	1 month up front		200				
Total Costs							
Closing balance							

Figure 16.1: Cashflow Statement - showing cashflow for costs incurred in March

Notes on the cashflow statement (figure 16.1):

- the opening balance for each month is the brought forward amount from the previous month's closing balance
- depending on the type of business the sales income could be up front, payment with purchase, or one, two or three months after a sale is made - in this example there is one month credit
- office rent is one month in advance
- heating, lighting and water authorities give one month credit
- telephone, Internet and other communication costs give you one month credit
- professional fees and consultants give two months credit
- bank charges and credit card payments give one month credit
- wages and salaries are paid in the same month the work is carried out
- material costs could include a range of terms - in this case one month credit
- equipment costs could include a range of terms - in this case two months up-front
- transport costs could include a range of terms - in this case one month up-front.

Capital equipment, machinery and plant purchases can have a big impact on the cashflow, particularly if they are purchased as a lump sum. For this reason, capital equipment is often leased and paid for monthly, or financed separately from an investment account.

The build-up and clearing of stock can also have a huge impact on the company's cashflow figures. This will be discussed in the stocking and destocking section below.

The cashflow forecast gives a monthly snap shot of the amount of money coming in and going out of the company's bank account. Because of the differential timings of the costs and incomes this will paint a different picture to the accrual method. Most importantly the cashflow forecast gives an indication of the amount of working capital required (if any), when, and how much. This enables the entrepreneur to plan ahead.

The prospect of negative cashflow brings the entrepreneur's wheeler-dealer instincts into play. To iron out the negative cashflow the entrepreneur will try to negotiate with the stakeholders to speed up income payments, but will try and delay expense payments. If there is still a short fall of funds the entrepreneur will try to negotiate an overdraft facility from a bank.

2. Stocking and Destocking

"My business is growing every month with rocketing sales figures, but we always seem to be short of cash - Why?"

The cashflow forecast can also be used to show the differential cashflow impact caused by stocking and destocking. Stocking is the gearing up of materials and stock to supply increasing sales, while destocking is the winding down of stock as sales reduce.

Stocking Exercise 1: Consider the following situation where a company manufacturing machines has a steady sales turnover of six machines each month. In the steady state the cashflow forecast would be the same each month showing a profit of $20,000 per month. Now let us make the situation a little more complicated - the sales from April increase to ten machines per month. Using the timing of the costs and income below, calculate the cashflow forecast for April, May, June, July and August.

Consider how the cashflow timing will change the cashflow forecast:
- Sales: $10,000 per machine, 3 months credit.
- Overheads: $4,000 per month, paid in the month of use.
- Labour: $5,000 per machine, paid in the month of work.
- Raw material: $1,000 per machine, 1 month credit

	Costs	Timing	Mar	Apr	May	Jun	Jul	Aug
Sales Units			6	10	10	10	10	10
Income	$10,000	3 m	60,000	60,000	60,000	60,000	100,000	100,000
Overheads	$4,000	0 m	4,000	4,000	4,000	4,000	4,000	4,000
Labour	$5,000	0 m	30,000	50,000	50,000	50,000	50,000	50,000
Material	$1,000	1 m	6,000	6,000	10,000	10,000	10,000	10,000
Profit			20,000	0	-4,000	-4,000	36,000	36,000

Figure 16.2: Stocking Cashflow Statement - showing the impact of increased sales

Although the sales increase in April, the income remains the same for three months because of the three months credit. The overheads remain the same as they are independent of sales figures, but the labour costs increase immediately as the workers are paid each month. The material costs increase in May as the suppliers give one month credit. The bottom line is that although the sales figures increase, initially the cashflow reduces to zero and then goes into negative figures for two months until the increased income kicks in. Once this happens, there is a healthy cash surplus of $36,000 per month.

Destocking Exercise 2: Now consider the impact on the cashflow when the sales in September reduce back to six machines per month.

	Costs	Timing	Aug	Sept	Oct	Nov	Dec	Jan
Sales	Units		10	6	6	6	6	6
Income	$10,000	3 m	100,000	100,000	100,000	100,000	60,000	60,000
Overheads	$4,000	0 m	4,000	4,000	4,000	4,000	4,000	4,000
Labour	$5,000	0 m	50,000	30,000	30,000	30,000	30,000	30,000
Material	$1,000	1 m	10,000	10,000	6,000	6,000	6,000	6,000
Profit			36,000	56,000	60,000	60,000	20,000	20,000

Figure 16.3: Destocking Cashflow Statement - showing the impact of reduced sales

Surprise! The reduced sales have a miraculous impact on the cashflow. The cashflow immediately increases to $56,000 in September and $60,000 in October and November, until the reduced sales figures kick in, and then in December, the monthly profit reduces back to $20,000 per month.

Small business entrepreneurs need to be aware of the stocking and destocking impact on the cashflow. New ventures with up-front costs will have a negative impact on cashflow, so funds need to be available to tide the business over this phase. Further, the buyer of a business needs to be aware that if the seller is destocking this could have a misleading positive impact on the latest sales figures.

Exercises:

1. Show how you would use a cashflow forecast in your business.

2. How can you negotiate better terms to address the impact of differential cashflows on your business?

3. Show how stocking and destocking could impact on your monthly cashflow figures.

Instructor's Manual: An Instructor's Manual is available with additional exercises and case studies, see <www.knowledgezone.net>.

17
Breakeven Point Analysis

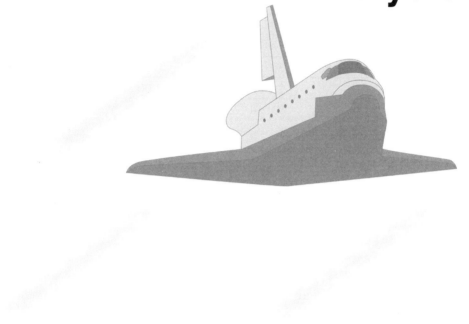

The breakeven point analysis and the payback period are two important financial calculations which give the entrepreneur a feel for the venture's exposure to risk and uncertainty. The breakeven point analysis calculates the number of units the company must sell to cover the set up costs (also called sunk costs), and the payback period calculates the time to get there. These figures are particularly important for products that initially consume a large amount of resources before making a profit.

To calculate the breakeven point the entrepreneur needs to subdivide the expenses into '*fixed costs*', '*variable costs*' and '*contribution per unit sale*' - as follows:

Fixed costs comprise of set up and overhead type costs (design, model testing, machinery, office rent, salaries, marketing etc.), and would typically be one off costs to establish the product. By their nature, fixed costs are incurred whether any products are manufactured or not. Fixed costs are shown as a horizontal line in figure 17.1.

Variable costs comprise of the cost of actually making the product. The costs are variable in the sense that they increase with the number of units manufactured, and are only incurred when the product is manufactured. This would obviously include labour, materials and variable overheads (electricity and heating). Assuming the cost of making each unit can be averaged out to be the same, the '*variable costs*' can be represented by a diagonal line as shown in figure 17.1. Note this calculation has not considered any economy of scale - in practice one would expect the unit cost to reduce as the production run increases.

The **income** is from the sales turnover. The income increases with increased unit sales and is shown as a diagonal line in figure 17.1. The breakeven point is reached when the sales income equals the combined total of fixed costs and variable costs.

The **contribution per unit sale** is the amount available to repay the fixed costs after the variable costs have been deducted from the income - as follows:

Contribution per unit sales = Income per unit sales - variable costs

The **breakeven point** can also be calculated by dividing the '*contribution per unit sales*' into the '*fixed costs*' - as follows:

Breakeven point = Fixed Costs
                 ———————————————
                 Contribution per unit sales

You can now see why you need to calculate separately the '*fixed costs*', '*variable costs*', '*sales income*' and '*contribution per unit sale*'.

Breakeven Example 1: A company makes a product which they sell for $15 each. The variable cost to make the product is $5 per unit, this covers the direct labour, direct material and the direct overhead costs to make the product, leaving $10 per unit as a contribution towards the fixed costs. The fixed costs total is $75,000 which covers all the sunk costs for the design, equipment and set up costs. The breakeven point is reached when the contribution per unit sale equals the fixed costs.

Breakeven point = Fixed Costs
                ———————————————
                Contribution per unit sale
                = $75,000   = 7,500 units
                  ————————
                  $10

The breakeven point is 7,500 units, this is when the sales income equals the total cost of $112,500 (labour and material 7,500 x 5 = $37,500) + (fixed costs of $75,000). Output less than this amount would make a loss, while an output more than this amount would make a profit. This profit or loss situation can be easily read off a graph, or calculated directly.

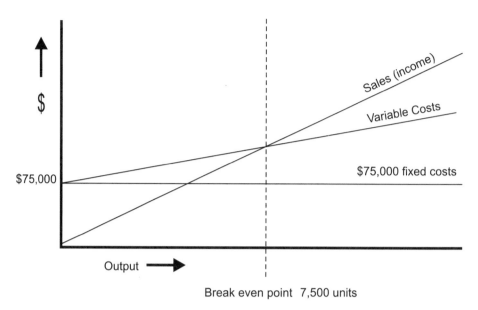

Figure 17.1: Breakeven Point Analysis - showing the breakeven point at the intersection of the sales (income) and the combined value of the fixed costs and the variable costs

1. Product Lifecycle Cashflow Curve

The product lifecycle looks at the big picture - from the cradle to the grave! Figure 17.2 shows how the product lifecycle can be subdivided into a project lifecycle to set up and develop a product or facility, followed by the operational phase to make the product, and finally ending with the disposal phase.

The **resultant cashflow line** is the difference between the income and expenditure - as follows:

Resultant Cashflow = Income - Expenditure

If the cashflow is superimposed on the product lifecycle the resultant cashflow will initially be negative as the funds are used to set up and develop the product or facility, but as the product moves into manufacture and sales, so the resultant cashflow curve bottoms out and starts to progress upwards. The breakeven point is reached when the resultant cashflow curve crosses the zero baseline.

As the product's sales continue to grow, so the cash surplus steadily increases. In the long term, the typical sales profile will reach a peak then slowly fall off. As the sales decline, so the resultant cashflow will decline until the management decides to dispose of the product.

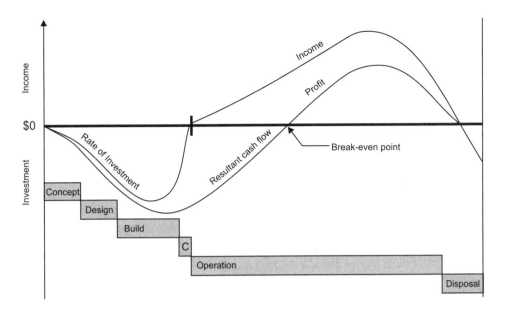

Figure 17.2: Product Lifecycle Cashflow - showing the project lifecycle subdivided into the concept, design, build and commissioning phases. The breakeven point is where the resultant cashflow line crosses the zero baseline

Exercises:

1. Calculate the breakeven point for one of your products.
2. Show how the payback period relates to risk management.
3. Draw the product lifecycle cashflow for one of your products.

Instructor's Manual: An Instructor's Manual is available with additional exercises and case studies, see <www.knowledgezone.net>.

18
Cash Book

Wouldn't it be nice to hand over all the bookkeeping to an accountant and tell them to get on with it - well you can! Following on from the discussion in the previous chapters, the small business entrepreneur tries to work very closely with his accountant, bank manager and other funding stakeholders. This enables the entrepreneur to focus on his key competitive advantage - which is not bookkeeping!

This chapter will discuss the format of the cash book and the balance sheet which are used in conjunction with the other financial statements discussed in the previous chapters.

1. Cash Book

The cash book method captures all the financial transactions for the period and logs them in a structured data base - it is from this data base that other accounting documents draw their raw data (for example, the cashflow forecast, breakeven point analysis, payback period, balance sheet etc.). Compiling the cash book is the starting point for many small businesses, and in some cases the cash book method actually forms the backbone of their accounting system.

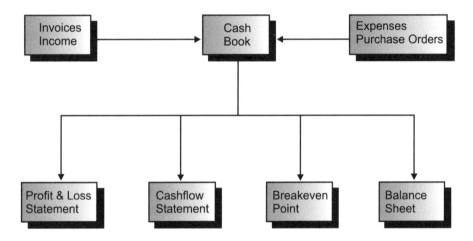

Figure 18.1: Cash Book Accounting System - showing the income and expense information, and a number of the standard reports which can be drawn from the information

Date	Purchase Order	Supplier	Description	Amount Paid	Date Paid
1 June 2007	P1008	BOC	LPG	£1000	1 July 2007
2 June 2007	P1009	Staples	Stationery	£500	2 June 2007
3 June	P1010	BT	Telephone	£100	1 July 2007

Figure 18.2: Cash Book - format for expense information

The cash book expense headings are set out to summarise and control the payments of expenses. The headings in figure 18.2 are typical of a simple cash book format. The headings are shown here as a guide to help you understand the cash book concept and indicate where more fields can be added for more information and control.

Date: The date field states the date the purchase order is raised. This enables the expenses to be sorted in date order.

Purchase Order: The purchase order number field links the purchase order (or transaction number / cheque number) to the company's budget, the supplier's quotation and the supplier's invoice. It is important to have an easy method to confirm that the invoice relates to the quotation. This can be achieved by adding additional fields to flag any variance.

Supplier: The supplier field identifies the company that supplied the goods, and enables the goods to be sorted by supplier. When dealing with a supplier it is useful to be able to quickly list all their deliveries.

Description: The description of the goods or service field helps to identify the expenses. The description field also enables all the goods of the same description to be grouped together. This could be useful if you have used a number of different suppliers.

Amount Paid: The amount paid field enables a comparison between the amount paid with the purchase order, the quotation and the budget. Another field can be added to show the VAT which is an essential component of bookkeeping. It is important to have an easy method to ensure the payment is not greater than the invoice.

Date Paid: The date invoice paid field enables you to confirm the payment has been made.

Date	Invoice Number	Customer	Invoice Amount	Amount Received	Date Received
1 June 2007	07-1001	Virgin	£10,000	£10,000	25 June 2007
1 June 2007	07-1002	Microsoft	£2,000	£2,000	2 July 2005
1 June 2007	07-1003	Enron	£5,000	£4,000	10 October 2007

Figure 18.3: Cash Book - format for income information

The cash book income headings are set out to summarise and control the client's payments. The headings in figure 18.3 are shown as a guide to demonstrate the cash book concept, and indicate where more fields can be added.

Date: The date of invoice field sorts the invoices into date order. This field is required to structure the 30, 60 and 90 day statements, and identify any late payments which require further action.

Invoice Number: The invoice number field links the invoice to the work (job number), the company's budget and the clients purchase order.

Customer: The customer field identifies the customer and enables you to sort by customer. By grouping all the invoices per customer, this will enable further analysis. For example, if a customer is late paying an invoice you might want to investigate to see if they were late paying any previous invoices.

Invoice Amount: The invoice amount field shows the amount of the invoice. Another field can be added to show the VAT which is an essential component of bookkeeping.

Amount Received: The amount received field confirms the invoice has been paid in full.

Date Received: The date received field shows the date the invoice was paid. Adding another field for the time to pay the invoice (Invoice Date - Date Received) will enable you to quickly identify any customer who consistently pay their invoices late.

Variances: A variance is the difference between two numbers. As mentioned above additional fields can be added to measure the variance between key figures, this enables a management by exception (MBE) approach. For example, if two key fields differed by more than 5%, or say £1000, this could automatically be brought to your attention.

2. Balance Sheet

The balance sheet, also called statement of financial position, is a snapshot of the balance between the company's assets and the company's liabilities on any particular day. For management purposes the balance sheet can be presented as a two column format of assets and liabilities (figure 18.4), or as a one column format with the figures from previous years to show any trends (figure 18.5).

ASSETS		LIABILITIES	
1. Fixed Assets		3. Capital	
Property	$500,000	Shareholders Capital	$600,000
Plant, Machinery, Vehicles	$500,000	Retained Earnings	$200,000
TOTAL FIXED ASSETS	$1,000,000	TOTAL CAPITAL	$800,000
		4. Term Liabilities	
		Loans	$100,000
2. Current Assets	$	5. Current Liabilities	
Cash in Hand (Bank)	$50,000	Bank Overdraft	$0
Stock	$100,000	Tax Payable	$60,000
Debtors	$50,000	Creditors	$240,000
TOTAL CURRENT ASSETS	$200,000	TOTAL LIABILITIES	$300,000
TOTAL ASSETS	$1,200,000	TOTAL CAPITAL & LIABILITIES	$1,200,000

Figure 18.4: Balance Sheet - two column format balancing assets and liabilities

1. Fixed Assets: Fixed assets are items of a permanent nature that will be part of the business for a long period of time. Fixed assets include all the capital items in the business, even items which have not yet been paid for (unpaid amounts will be included in liabilities under creditors).

2. Current Assets: A balance sheet is normally based on actual figures at the reported date. This includes actual cash in hand (bank), actual amounts owed (debtors), and actual stock in hand even if the stock has not yet been paid for (unpaid stock will appear as a liability under creditors).

3. Capital: On the liabilities side of the balance sheet enter as shareholders capital the amount of money you have invested in the business. From the retained earning enter the forecast profit for the period. If you forecast a loss, enter the figure in brackets () as a deduction from your capital.

	2007	2006	2005
1. Fixed Assets			
Property	$500,000		
Plant, Machinery, Vehicles	$500,000		
TOTAL FIXED ASSETS	$1,000,000		
2. Current Assets			
Bank Accounts	$50,000		
Stock	$100,000		
Debtors	$50,000		
TOTAL CURRENT ASSETS	$200,000		
3. Capital			
Shareholders Capital	$600,000		
Retained Earnings	$200,000		
TOTAL CAPITAL	$800,000		
4. Term Liabilities			
Loans	$100,000		
5. Current Liabilities			
Bank Overdraft	$0		
Tax Payable	$60,000		
Creditors	$240,000		
TOTAL LIABILITIES	**$300,000**		

Figure 18.5: Balance Sheet - with additional columns to show historical information

4. Term Liabilities: Term liabilities are loans which are not due to be repaid within the current year.

5. Current Liabilities: Include bank overdrafts, tax payable (include VAT) and trade creditors. The bank overdraft and the creditors can be taken from the cashflow forecast and the tax payable can be taken from the profit and loss statement.

Bottom Line: The bottom line of the balance sheet must balance - the total liabilities must equal the total assets. If there is a difference check your figures to ensure all balances have been included.

Historical Analysis: With the one column balance sheet you can show figures from the last few years. The historical figures enable you to identify trends which may be more important than the actual numbers.

19
Red Tape

Governments are always criticised by small business associations for being too bureaucratic and over regulating the economy with unnecessary rules and regulations which stifle small business development. The small business lobby argues that, for a country to achieve economic growth, it must establish a healthy small business environment that encourages entrepreneurship and small business enterprise.

In response to these criticisms the British government has actually said, "*We want to make Britain the best place in the world to set up a business*". But what do they mean by '*best place*'?

1. Best Place To Do Business

A good place to do business is usually associated with the following:

- ease of setting up a company
- ease of raising finance
- ease of enforcing a contract
- ease of hiring and firing workers
- lack of red tape and unnecessary rules and regulations
- low business compliance costs.

Each of these points will be discussed before discussing the consequence of red tape and the black market.

Ease of Setting up a Company: This is usually quantified as the time and cost to register a company. The time to register a company is quantified in days, and the cost of registering a company is quantified in dollars, and then expressed as a percentage of the local annual income. Ease of registering a company is influenced by the number of people and number of departments you have to contact, where they are located (are they in the same building or the other side of town?), and if you need to go there in person.

The ease of setting up a company is further influenced by the number of procedures to register a company, such as the number of forms to fill in. These requirements can be eased somewhat if they can be handled by an agent, for which, of course, there would be a fee (see figure 19.1: **Doing Business Database** for more information).

Ease of Raising Finance: Entrepreneurs thrive when they have access to funds to finance the development of their new ventures. The funds could be in the form of personal savings, loans from family, friends and banks, or equity investments from business angels and venture capital firms. There might also be support in the form of government grants, soft loans, tax breaks and sponsored assistance from incubators and science parks.

The banks are becoming far more understanding of the small business entrepreneur's financial needs, as they themselves are having to compete for clients from the small business sector.

Ease of Enforcing a Contract: Ease of enforcing a contract is well established in the West and, with the small claims courts, the process is quick and inexpensive. However, with increasing outsourcing offshore, the small business entrepreneur will be brought into contact with other legal systems.

Ease of Hiring and Firing Workers: Government employment regulations are often counter productive as they result in a delicate balance between employees' and employers' rights. Allowing the pendulum to swing too far in favour of the employee could actually reduce the number of jobs available!

Easing employment regulations usually encourages companies to employ as many workers as possible with the understanding that they will be able to reduce their workforce to match any down turns in demand in the economy.

Economist: *'Jobs are so thickly protected that employers hesitate to create them. Many resort to temporary or short-term contracts, or to interns. The upshot is a two-tier labour market: sheltered jobs for those who have them, and precariousness or joblessness for the rest.'*

Lack of Red Tape: Red tape is the administration of government paperwork and procedures that are both time consuming and costly to businesses, particularly small businesses. The term red tape is derived from early business practice when government paperwork was bound with red strands.

Low Business Compliance Costs: Business compliance costs comprise of the time and money spent within the enterprise complying with rules, regulations and statutory requirements. These could be;
- tax requirements [VAT and PAYE]
- employment-related requirements
- environment-related requirements
- the cost of external advice.

These costs are disproportionately more onerous for the smaller companies because the overhead costs can only be written off over a few employees, which means the smallest companies are the hardest hit.

2. Doing Business Database

The **Doing Business Database** is produced by the **World Bank** to provide objective measures of business regulations and their enforcement. The Doing Business indicators are compared across 145 economies. They indicate the regulatory compliance costs of businesses and can be used to analyse how specific regulations enhance or constrain investment, productivity and growth.

Figure 19.1 shows the data from a selection of countries, for the complete data base see www.rru.worldbank.org/doingbusiness.

Country	Procedures	Time (days)	Cost (US$)	Cost (% of income per capita)	Min capital (% of income per capita)
Angola	14	146	5531	838	174
Australia	2	2	402	2	0
Brazil	15	152	331	11.6	0
Canada	2	3	127	0.6	0
Congo	13	215	785	872	321
Ecuador	14	90	914	63	28
Indonesia	11	168	103	15	303
Kenya	11	61	104	54	0
New Zealand	3	3	28	0.2	0
Papua New Guinea	7	69	140	26	0
Saudi Arabia	14	95	10,814	131	1561
South Africa	9	38	227	9	0
UK	6	18	264	1	0
USA	5	4	210	0.6	0

Figure 19.1 Doing Business Data Base (World Bank)

Note the difference between the countries in the West and the countries in the Third World. The time to register a company in the West is less than a week (except for the UK!), whereas in the Third World it can take months (a staggering 215 days in the Congo). Note the cost of registering a company in the West is 1% or 2% of income per capita, whereas in the Third World it can be over 800%. In the West there is no minimum capital required, whereas in the Third World it is over 100% of per capita income. With these extreme requirements the average person in the Third World is highly unlikely to be able to register a company.

The findings from the World Bank's Doing Business Database indicate that in countries where the regulatory burden is highest so the black economy is the most proactive - this would seem to be a natural instinctive reaction by the local people out of necessity, in order to survive.

It may come as a surprise to discover that it is the poorest countries that have the most overpowering red tape; one would have thought that the poorest countries would encourage small business enterprise to raise their standard of living. Perhaps it was the red tape that put them there in the first place!

3. Green Economy

The trading and **bartering** of goods is often referred to as the 'green economy' so named after the agricultural sector. Traditionally farmers have traded their products with other farmers who are producing a different product. For example, a farmer growing potatoes may trade a bag of potatoes for a box of apples. Bartering means you trade something you have for something you want, and so remove the need for cash. But going shopping in a hypermarket with a wheelbarrow of farm products is not the most convenient way to go shopping. (See Bartercard's web site for information on an international bartering network.)

If you think bartering is a good way of avoiding tax, you are unfortunately wrong. The next time you trade any products remember to pay the VAT and include it on your income statement!

4. The Black Market

The 'Black Market' is the term used to cover all the activities in the informal cash economy. In the West these would typically be cash jobs (usually domestic) and the supply of illegal products (drugs and stolen goods). In the developing economies the black market can actually be the largest sector of the economy and so form the backbone of the economy.

It is generally thought that governments are against black market activities because they are not able to generate any tax revenue from the work and transactions. The governments say that, as the size of the black market increases, this puts an unfair tax burden on the people and companies that **do** pay their taxes. This is particularly evident in countries such as Russia, where the black market accounts for a massive 60% of the economy. There are a number of other sound economic reasons why the black market works against the long term benefit of the economy. Consider the following:

- lower street prices for goods might be good for the consumer, but it usually means lower salaries for the workers, particularly for people who are desperate for work (women and children in sweat shops)
- people who work illegally, for example those working without work permits, do not have the protection of the law (because they are not going to tell the police they are working without a work permit!). This situation plays right into the hands of unscrupulous employers
- working illegally means the informal sector does not have the protection of the courts - broken contracts and bad debts cannot be sorted out legally (this is where the heavies come in). This sort of environment stifles business investment and growth

- unregistered businesses that do all their transactions in cash are unable to obtain credit from banks because they are not able to document their business dealings. This means they cannot gain financial investment leverage other than ploughing back the profits
- unregistered property and equity cannot be used to secure a loan
- black market companies generally feel they have an uncertain future and are, therefore, slow to hire workers. They are also reluctant to hire inexperienced workers who cannot produce the goods immediately. Needless to say, they do not offer apprenticeships, so do not supply the economy with a trained workforce.

Informal companies usually stay small because they want to fall under the authorities' radar. This means that, even if they had the funds, they would not invest in automated machinery because this might attract unwanted attention, even though this would lower their production costs, expand their market and increase their profit.

From time to time governments try and legitimise the black market with incentives and amnesties, but who are they fooling? The reality is that with every law the government passes; whether it be minimum wage, working hours, employment rights, Health and Safety, building regulations or maternity leave; they all make going 'unofficial' more attractive. The Doing Business Database confirms a direct relationship between red tape bureaucracy and the black market.

Exercises:

1. Can you put a dollar value on the cost of complying with unnecessary red tape (include a value for your time).

2. Have you ever asked "*How much for cash*?". What happened next?

3. What products could you barter?

Instructor's Manual: An Instructor's Manual is available with additional exercises and case studies, see <www.knowledgezone.net>.

Glossary of Terms

Accounts: Business accounts can have two meanings. It can mean the expenses and invoices of the business. Or it can mean the financial records of the business including the cashflow statement, the profit and loss statement, and the balance sheet.

Accounts (Shoe Box): Implies a small number of transactions which can all be contained in a shoe box under the bed.

Assets: An asset is anything of worth that a person or business owns. These can be subdivided into current assets and fixed assets. Current assets include cash in-hand, money in the bank, stock and money owed to you by customers. Fixed assets are items of a permanent nature which include office equipment, plant and machinery.

B2B (Business-to-Business): Trade between businesses.

Balance Sheet: Is a financial 'snapshot' of your business at a given time (usually at the end of the financial year). It lists your assets, your liabilities and the difference between the two, which are your equity or net worth. Where assets = liabilities + owner's equity.

Black Market: Refers to the informal sector, cash-in-hand jobs, usually domestic jobs.

Breakeven Point: The number of units you have to sell to cover the set up costs - after this you start to make a profit.

Cash Book: Collates and documents all the business transactions into a cash book.

Cashflow: The actual movement of money within a business. The cashflow predicts how much cash is needed and when it is needed. Cashflow forecasts are usually presented monthly.

Company (Limited): A legal entity that is separate from its owners. Companies are registered and must operate in accordance with company laws. Liability of each shareholder is restricted to the amount of their actual investment in the business.

Compliance Costs: The cost of complying with government rules and regulations (red tape).

Credit: Another word for debt. Credit is given to customers when they are allowed to make a purchase with the promise to pay later. A bank gives credit when it lends money.

Credit Control: Collecting payments from your customers.

Creditor: Someone who gives you credit. Someone you owe money to.

Debit: Money owed to you (opposite to credit).

Debtor: Someone who owes a debit. Someone who owes you money.

Depreciation: A decrease in value through age, wear or deterioration. Depreciation is accepted as a normal business expense.

Deregulation: Removing rules and regulations, particularly those which limit the free enterprise of small businesses and entrepreneurship.

Disaster Recovery Planning: Contingency planning to enable the business to survive a disaster, for example, relating to the recovery of information caused by a computer failure or virus.

Distribution: The process of moving a product within the supply chain.

Enterprise: A venture characterized by innovation, creative thinking, dynamism, and risk.

Entrepreneur: Is an innovator of business enterprise who recognizes opportunities to introduce a new product, raises the necessary money, assembles the resources for production and organizes a new venture to exploit the opportunity.

Equity: The net worth of your business. A financial investment in a business. An equity investment carries with it a share of ownership of the business, a stake in the profits and a say in how it is managed. Equity is calculated by subtracting the liabilities of the business from the assets of the business.

Estimating: Uses estimating techniques to predict future costs and incomes.

Feasibility Study: An investigation into a proposed venture to confirm it will work, confirm there is a market, and ensure it is making the best use of the entrepreneur's resources.

Franchise: An agreement enabling the franchisee to sell or provide a product or service owned by the manufacturer or supplier (franchisor). The franchise is regulated by a franchise agreement that specifies the terms and conditions of the franchise. The franchise fee usually includes management systems, equipment, training and support.

Franchisee: The person who buys the rights from the franchisor to operate the franchise business.

Franchisor: The person who sells the rights to the franchisee to operate the franchise business.

Funding: Money required to set up and run a business.

Goodwill: An intangible business asset which gives value to the customers' loyalty to continue buying the business' goods and services.

Liability: A liability is something you owe (a debt) or a claim against your assets for a guarantee you may have given as a director or trustee.

Mentor: Experienced person who can guide you through the small business entrepreneurial process.

Networking: Your connections who can help your business with information and the free use of their resources to enhance your competitive advantage. To be enduring, this help needs to be reciprocated by sharing of your information.

Offshoring: Outsourcing work to an overseas company (typically back office and call-centers to India and manufacturing to China).

Outsourcing: The term used when a product or service task which has previously been carried out within the company (an inside source), is now being purchased from another company (an outside source). It usually refers to non-core activities which can be performed cheaper by an outside company that specialises in that line of work. Outsourcing also reduces operational costs and capital expenditure.

Partnership: When two or more people set up a business together. Partnerships benefit from the interaction and complementary skills of the members. However, this needs to be balanced with the risk of each partner being liable for all the partnership debts and unpaid taxes.

Payback Period: The time it takes to reach the breakeven point, or the length of time it will take for an investor to recoup the set up costs.

Profit and Loss Statement: Collates the incomes and expenses of a product, and calculates the bottom line; whether the product will make a profit or loss for the business.

Project Management: The management technique used to plan and control a new venture.

Red Tape: Unnecessary bureaucracy, particularly relating to the time and cost to comply with rules and regulations. A common name applied to procrastination and confusing language that invariably occurs in most large organizations. This lack of clarity and excessive paperwork usually causes delays.

Shareholder: Person who owns equity in a company.

SME: Small and Medium Enterprise - 0 to 250 employees.

Sole Trader: A form of business ownership in which one person owns the entire business, earns all the profits and assumes all the losses.

Stocking (Destocking): Stocking is the buying of products to increase the stock available. This can have a huge negative impact on the cashflow until the sales income comes rolling in. Destocking is the reverse process which can have a positive impact on the cashflow.

SWOT Analysis: Quantifies your present strengths and weaknesses, and your future opportunities and threats.

Telemarketing: Advertising, canvassing or selling over the telephone.

Variance: The difference between two numbers. In financial accounting it is the difference between actual expenses and the budgeted amount.

Warehousing: A warehouse is a building used to store merchandise or other materials or equipment. Warehousing usually involves storing, stock control, inventory control and retrieval.

Book List

Ashton, Robert. (2004), *The Entrepreneur's Book of Checklists*, Pearson

Bolton, W. and **Thompson**, B.K. (2003), *Entrepreneurs in Focus,* Thomson

Bolton, W.K. and **Thompson**, J.L. (2000), *Entrepreneurs - Talent, Temperament, Technique*, Butterworth Heinemann

Burke, Rory. (2003), *Project Management Planning and Control Techniques (4ed)*, Burke Publishing

Burke, Rory. (2006), *Entrepreneurs Toolkit*, Burke Publishing

Burke, Rory. (2006), *Small Project Entrepreneur*, Burke Publishing

Burke, Rory. (2006), *Team Building Entrepreneur*, Burke Publishing

Burns, Paul. (2001), *Entrepreneurship and Small Business*, Palgrave Macmillan

Bygrave, W.D. (2004), *Portable MBA Entrepreneurship*, John Wiley

Carter, Sara, and **Jones-Evans**, Dylan. *Enterprise and Small Business*, FT Prentice Hall

Chaston, Ian. (2000), *Entrepreneurial Marketing*, Macmillan Business

Chell, E. *Entrepreneurship: Globalisation, Innovation and Development*, Thomson

Deakins, D. and **Freel**, Mark. (2003), *Entrepreneurship and Small Firms*, McGraw-Hill

Foley, James. (1999), *The Global Entrepreneur*, Dearborn

Frederick, H. and **Kuratko**, D. (2006). *Australasian Entrepreneurship: Theory, Practice and Process.* Thomson Learning

Green, Jim. *Starting Your Own Business,* How To Books

Hall, David. (1999), *In The Company of Heroes*, Kogan Page

Harvard Business Essential. (2005), *Entrepreneur's Toolkit*, HBS Press

Hisrich, Robert, and **Peter**, Michael. *Entrepreneurship* (5ed), McGraw-Hill

Kirby, David. *Entrepreneurship,* McGraw-Hill

Lang, Jack. (2002), *The High-Tech Entrepreneur's Handbook*, FT.com

Legge, John, and **Hindle**, Kevin. (2004), *Entrepreneurship Context, Vision and Planning*, Palgrave Macmillan

Morris, Michael. *Successful Expansion for the Small Business*, Kogan Page

Morris, Michael. *The Sunday Times Guide to Starting a Successful Business*, Kogan Page

Darling, Diane. (2003), *Networking Survival Guide*, McGraw-Hill

Oliver, Leith, and **English**, John. (2002), *Small Business Book*, Bridget Williams Books

Rae, D. *The Entrepreneurial Spirit: Learning to Unlock Value*, Blackhall

Roddick, Anita. (2002), *Business As Unusual*, Thorsons

Senior, Glen, and **McBride**, Ian. (2000), *Small Business Survival Tactics*, Enterprise Publications

Sibbald, Peter. (2005), *Slash Your Compliance Costs*, Reed Business

Stone, Phil. *Your Own Business: The Complete Guide to Succeeding With a Small Business*, How To Books

Sugars, Brad. (2002), *Billionaire in Training*, Action International

Susac, Kristina. (2004), *Successful Selling*, Duncan Baird Publishers

Waterworth, D. *Marketing for the Small Business*, Macmillan

Wickham, P.A. *Strategic Entrepreneurship,* Prentice Hall

Williams, Sara. (2003), *Lloyds TSB Small Business Guide*, Penguin

Index

Fashion Design Series

This *Fashion Design Series* promotes fashion design skills and techniques which can be effectively applied in the world of fashion.

Fashion Computing – Computer Techniques and CAD
Sandra Burke, ISBN: 0-9582391-3-4

This book introduces you to the computer drawing and design skills required by the fashion industry worldwide. Through visuals and easy steps, it explains how to use the most popular graphics software used in the fashion business. It demonstrates fashion drawing, design and presentation techniques and explains how to develop digital communications using powerful computerised tools.

Fashion Artist - Drawing Techniques to Portfolio Presentation
Sandra Burke, ISBN: 0-473-05438-8

Fashion drawing is an essential part of the fashion designer's portfolio of skills. This book is set out as a self-learning programme to teach you how to draw fashion figures and clothing, and present them in a portfolio. The text is supported with explanatory drawings and photographs, together with drawing exercises and worked solutions to speedily aid the learning process.

Fashion Design – Catwalk to Street
Sandra Burke, ISBN: 0-9582391-2-6 (2007)

This book will help you develop your portfolio of fashion design skills while guiding you through the fashion design process. Starting with the design brief, it explains how to analyse fashion trends, develop a collection, choose fabrics and colorways, create sketchbooks, flats and design presentations. It essentially takes you from concept to creation, and catwalk to street.

www.burkepublishing.com

Bluewater Trilogy

Be warned - this *Bluewater Trilogy* will inspire you to give it all up to go Bluewater Cruising!

Managing Your Bluewater Cruise

Rory and Sandra Burke, ISBN: 0-473-03822-6, 352 pages

This **preparation guide** discusses a range of pertinent issues from establishing budgets and buying equipment to preventative maintenance and heavy weather sailing. The text works closely with the ORC category 1 requirements and includes many comments from other cruisers who are '*out there doing it*'. So if you wish to bridge the gap between fantasy and reality then your bluewater cruise must be effectively managed.

Greenwich to the Dateline

Rory and Sandra Burke, ISBN: 0-620-16557-x, 352 pages

This is a **travelogue** of our bluewater cruising adventure from the Greenwich Meridian to the International Dateline – sit back with a sundowner and be inspired to cruise to the Caribbean and Pacific islands. In this catalogue of rewarding experiences we describe how we converted our travelling dreams into a bluewater cruising reality.

Bluewater Checklist

Rory and Sandra Burke, ISBN: 0-9582391-0-X, 96 pages

Checklists provide an effective management tool to confirm everything is on board, and all tasks are completed. Why try to remember everything in your head when checklists never forget!!! This book provides a comprehensive portfolio of checklists covering every aspect of bluewater cruising.

www.burkepublishing.com

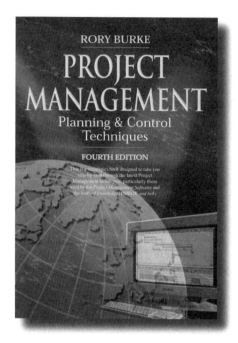

Project Management Planning and Control Techniques (4ed)

Rory Burke
ISBN: 0-9582391-5-0
384 pages

In our competitive world the successful manager needs Entrepreneurship skills to spot opportunities, and Project Management skills to make-it-happen.

Despite the advances in project management software, a project manager still needs to understand the basic principles of project management to apply the software successfully.

This book offers a structured approach to managing large and small projects. At some point in most projects you need integrated planning and control systems to guide you through a complex flood of data, conflicting problems, creative opportunities and multi-disciplined teams.

This book presents the latest planning and control techniques, particularly those used by the project management software and the body of knowledge. With sales of 100,000 copies, this book has established itself internationally as the standard text for project management techniques.

Greek translation
Rory Burke
ISBN: 960-218-289-X

The 2004 Olympic Games clearly showed the importance of effective planning and control to meet a fixed end date.

German translation
Rory Burke

ISBN: 3-8266-1443-7

Project management techniques are perfect for a country renowned for its precise time keeping and production quality.

Chinese translation
Rory Burke
ISBN: 0-471-98762-X

With the boom in demand for Chinese manufacturing, so there is an associated boom in Chinese infrastructure projects.

Cosmic MBA Series

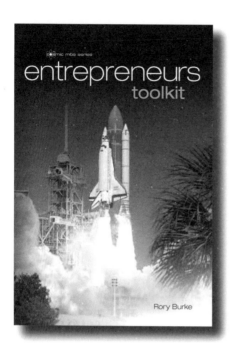

Entrepreneurs Toolkit
Rory Burke
ISBN: 0-9582391-4-2
160 pages

Entrepreneurs Toolkit is a comprehensive guide outlining the essential entrepreneur skills to spot a marketable opportunity, the essential business skills to start a new venture and the essential management skills to make-it-happen.

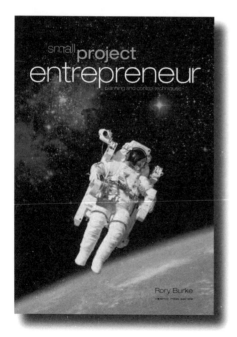

Small Project Entrepreneur
Rory Burke
ISBN: 0-9582391-1-8
160 pages

Small Project Entrepreneur is a comprehensive guide outlining the essential project management skills to plan and control a small project.

Cosmic MBA Series

Team Building Entrepreneur
Rory Burke
ISBN: 0-9582391-8-5
160 pages

Team Building Entrepreneur is a comprehensive guide outlining the essential leadership skills required to motivate and lead the team.

50 Plus Entrepreneur
Rory Burke
ISBN:
160 pages

50 Plus Entrepreneur is a comprehensive guide outlining how the 50 plus can use entrepreneurial skills to overcome employment blocks and age discrimination. Why continue working for someone else? This book will outline how to establish your own business and be in control of your lifestyle.

Lifestyle Entrepreneur

Rory Burke was educated at Wicklow and Oswestry. He has an MSc in Project Management (Henley) and degrees in Naval Architecture (Southampton) and Computer Aided Engineering (Coventry). Rory has worked on marine and offshore projects in Britain, South Africa, the Middle East and New Zealand.

After dreaming about bluewater cruising for twenty years, Rory finally decided to take the plunge and go for an entrepreneurial lifestyle. He discovered that the bluewater adventure made history and geography come alive as he followed in the footsteps of the great explorers.

The bluewater lifestyle has given Rory a sense of adventure where he feels he is living life to the full and allows him more time to focus on his research and writing. Where better to experience street entrepreneurs at source, where the first world meets the third world, and be able to negotiate with necessity entrepreneurs thriving in a black market economy.

To continue their bluewater lifestyle, Rory and Sandra have set up a publishing business, which they run from their yacht – a truly mobile office in the South Pacific.

To keep in touch with the 'real world', Rory is a visiting lecturer to universities in the UK, Australia, South Africa, Canada, America, Hong Kong and Singapore.

BBC interview

Rory Burke
M.Sc Project Management (Henley)